College Football's
Great Dynasties
ALABAMA

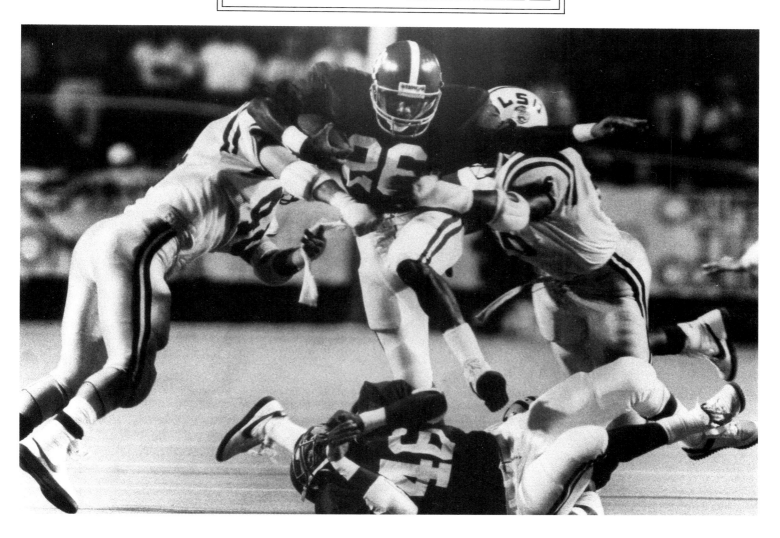

College Football's Great Dynasties

ALABAMA

Jack Clary

SMITHMARK

Published by Smithmark Publishers Inc.
112 Madison Avenue
New York, New York 10016

Produced by
Brompton Books Corp.
15 Sherwood Place
Greenwich, CT 06830

ISBN 0-8317-3475-2

Printed in Hong Kong

10 9 8 7 6 5 4 3 2 1

Previous pages:
*Running backs like
Bobby Humphrey*
(page 1), *a swarming
defense* **(page 2),** *and
diehard fans who
follow the team
everywhere* **(page 3)**
*have always been the
hallmarks of
Alabama football.*

These pages:
*Alabama's football
history includes more
bowl appearances
than any other team.
Here the 1937 team
prepares for the Rose
Bowl against
California.*

ACKNOWLEDGMENTS

The author must extend the warmest of Yankee
thanks to sports information director Larry White
and his staff at the University of Alabama for its
cooperation in helping compile so much of the material used in this book. Special thanks go to Ann Bar-
ron of that office for her time in digging up so much
material on Tide teams of the past. Also a gracious
note of acknowledgment goes to Mary Jane Craddock
of the Bear Bryant Museum in Tuscaloosa, who was
very diligent in her efforts to gather historical matter. Thanks also go to my dear friends Pat Harmon,
curator of the College Football Hall of Fame in Kings
Island, Ohio for his guidance in laying out this project; and Joe Horrigan, his counterpart at Pro Football's Hall of Fame, who also supplied some much-
needed research information. And of course, my
editor on this project, Jean Martin of the Bison Group
in Greenwich, Connecticut did her usual fine job of
presenting the project, adding encouragement, and
then standing back and letting it come together
before adding her own fine editing touch. Others who
deserve recognition for the preparation of this book
include Rita Longabucco, the picture editor; Don
Longabucco, the designer; and Elizabeth A. McCar-
thy, the indexer.

Jack Clary
Stow, Massachusetts

PHOTO CREDITS

All photographs courtesy of UPI/Bettmann
Newsphotos except the following:
Neil Brake: 6, 7, 62, 63(bottom), 65(top), 69(both),
    76, 77.
Chance Brockway: 53(left), 54(top left, bottom),
    57(top left), 58, 59, 60.
Brockway & Emmons: 56, 57(bottom), 61(top left),
    63(top), 68.
Malcolm Emmons: 64, 67(both).
Bruce Schwartzman: 2, 3, 57(top right), 61(bottom
    right).
University of Alabama: 8(top).
University of Alabama, W. S. Hoole Special
    Collections Library: 10, 11, 12, 13, 14-15(all five),
    16-17(all four), 36, 65(bottom).

Contents

Preface 6
1. Football Comes To The Capstone 10
2. The Tide Arrives 18
3. The Frank Thomas Era 26
4. Troubled Times 36
5. The Bear 42
6. The Tide Rolls On 56
7. Auburn Means War 64
8. 'Bama And The Bowls 70
Alabama Crimson Tide Football Records 78
Index 80

Preface

Say the words "Alabama football," and who comes to mind?

Bear Bryant, of course.

But Alabama football, nearly a century old, is more than Bryant, though no one did more to give the school's football program a measure of excellence during the quarter-century that he coached there than the late coach, who won 232 games at the Capstone. Long before Bryant, there was Wallace Wade, and Frank Thomas, and Red Drew . . . and long before them, there was Xen Scott and Doc Pollard . . . and with all of them came a group of athletes who were totally dedicated to being the very best for this grand old institution.

Football at Alabama is akin to a religious experience. There is no greater feeling than to be associated emotionally with a team, and a program, that has produced excellence during most of its existence. Alabama football is special; it is New Year's Day on

Right: *Alabama's famed "Red Elephant" mascot has been a symbol of its success since 1930.*

television, or in person, in bright, sunny climes with all the color and dazzle that bowl games can bring, as much as it is seeing scores of helmeted young men running onto the field at Bryant-Denny Stadium in Tuscaloosa, or Legion Field in Birmingham, with a sea of crimson and tens of thousands of spectators forming a storybook backdrop.

But long before the crowds form at those two great stadiums, or before bowl games begin, there is the constant image of a team wearing crimson jerseys and white numerals – a team often without great stars, but bonded to a mission of playing "Alabama Football."

There also are memories of players such as Johnny Mack Brown, who is remembered as much for his starring roles in west-

ern movies as for his exploits as one of the Crimson Tide's greatest. There was Dixie Howell, a marvelously gifted athlete who could run, pass (to a tremendously gifted end named Don Hutson), kick, and play some mean defense, and do it all better than anyone who ever played for Alabama. And there was Harry Gilmer, of the magical right arm, who as a freshman dazzled a nation that was seeking football heroes to replace those who had fought during World War II. Then, of course, there was Joe Namath, a gifted quarterback whose greatest fame came in professional football but who, even in his halcyon days as a cult hero of the 1960s, still had Alabama quietly inscribed on his heart.

And there are more: Ken Stabler; Steve Sloan; Pat Trammell; Johnny Musso;

Above: *Beating archrival Auburn is the ultimate triumph every season, and a reward often is an impromptu shower like the one coach Gene Stallings got after the Tide defeated the Tigers 16-7 in 1990.*

Walter Lewis; Bobby Humphrey, the school's all-time rushing leader; and two great linebackers of recent vintage, Cornelius Bennett and Derrick Thomas.

There is the unforgettable Tommy Lewis too, the young man who, in a blind act of passion for his school, once jumped off the bench and tackled an opposing runner, Dickie Moegle of Rice, to prevent him from scoring a touchdown in the Cotton Bowl game. He didn't stop the touchdown, but he made his own kind of football history.

And always, there seems to be Bryant, the bear of a man who even spoke (some said mumbled) in a low growl that was never menacing unless you weren't giving him your best effort as a player, or were foolishly denigrating his football team. As long as there will be Alabama football, there always will be Bryant's imposing shadow as an example of the excellence and dedication that it takes to become Number 1 and to remain Number 1.

Alabama built its football program long ago on the premise that a school can be successful in the classrooms and laboratories and still be successful on the gridiron. You don't even have to be an Alabama fan to acknowledge that that mission has been accomplished, and for that reason, above all else, the Crimson Tide has earned its niche as one of college football's greatest success stories.

Above: *Wallace Wade brought Alabama its first national recognition during his eight-season tenure from 1923 to 1930.*

Right: *Coach Frank Thomas turned out three unbeaten teams and two national champions, including his 1934 team, from 1931 to 1946.*

Above: *Paul (Bear) Bryant and Alabama football are forever linked because he won 232 games and six national championships in 25 seasons.*

Left: *Ray Perkins (catching ball) was a fine end at Alabama under Bear Bryant, and then succeeded him as head coach in 1983.*

1. Football Comes To The Capstone

In 1891 William G. Little, a stocky, curly black-haired youth from Livingston, Alabama, was attending Phillips-Exeter Academy in Andover, Massachusetts, a bucolic town of colonial vintage about 20 miles northwest of Boston. Then, as now, its primary aim was to prepare young students for ivy-encrusted universities such as Yale, where Little had planned to enroll the following year. While at Andover, Little had fallen in love with a new game called football. Yale's football captain and coach Walter Camp had reformed the earlier versions of this mixture of soccer and rugby by giving the game rules that made it unique. Young men being young men, it appealed to their instinctive desires to tussle with each other, to bump and to hit, to wrestle and to run deliberate collision courses that are their rites of passage.

Fate intervened, though, when a death in the family forced Little to return home to Alabama. So instead of Yale, the University of Alabama, with its 500 or so students at Tuscaloosa, became his college of choice. While his school loyalties changed, his fascination with and love of football remained steadfast, to the point that he even brought the tools of the game – his uniform, shoes, and a ball that none of his fellow students had ever seen – with him to school. His Alabama schoolmates became as intrigued as he had been at Andover, and when he suggested that they form a team, he had instant acceptance. Thus was born Alabama's great football heritage.

With its birth also came a big step toward maturity for athletics at Alabama. Baseball was already a popular sport, as were track and gymnastics, but when the University sanctioned a football team, it also formed its first Athletic Association. The team had enough players – and had elected Little as captain – but it needed a coach, and soon hired Eugene Beaumont, who had learned some of the game's basics while attending the University of Pennsylvania in Philadelphia, where the game had already begun to prosper. As he looked at his first team of eager young men, he had no idea that some of the school's most prominent alumni of the first half of the twentieth century stood before him. They included William Bankhead, later Speaker of the House of Representatives and father of renowned actress Tallulah Bankhead; Bibb Graves, a future two-term governor of the state and headed for a third term at the time of his death in 1942; Eli Abbott, a six-foot, one-inch tackle who was considered to be the school's greatest athlete in the last

W. B. BANKHEAD.

Left: *Yale's loss became Alabama football's biggest gain when William G. Little decided to return to his home state instead of attending the Ivy League school, enrolling at the Capstone and putting together the first team to become the "father of Alabama football."*

decade of the nineteenth century, and who also later became a very successful engineer; and others such as Robert E. Lee Cope, F. M. (Pops) Savage, Hub Kyser, Dan Smith, Tom Frazier, and Burr Ferguson.

At that time, though, the game was the thing; and while Little, who played as a guard, was the heftiest player at 220 pounds, the starting lineup averaged only 162 pounds. Only two others, H. M. Pratt and Abbott, who succeeded Beaumont as coach and held the job for three successive seasons (1893-95) and for a fourth season in 1903, were over six feet tall.

The first game was played at Lakeview Park in Birmingham on November 11, 1892

Below: *Eli Abbott was the star of Alabama's first football teams. He served as the Tide's coach from 1893-95, and again in 1903.*

against a selected group of high school players from that city. It was scheduled as a practice game for a battle the following day against the Birmingham Athletic Club, but University records still list it as the school's first football game, which the team won easily 56-0. The collegians scored 28 points in each half; the big plays were a 75-yard run by D. A. Grayson, one of 50 yards by Dan Smith and a 30-yard run by Little. Students wishing to leave the campus to watch it had to present written permission from their families. Most stayed to see Alabama suffer its first loss the next day, 5-4 — the last time Alabama would lose by a single point until a 21-20 loss to Tulane in 1947. Little scored the Tide's only touchdown but M. P. Walker missed the extra point, while the A.C.'s J. P. Ross was forever remembered for booting a mighty 63-yard field goal in the final minutes to win the game (field goals counted five

Left: *Alabama's first team poses for a group photo in 1892. Eugene Beaumont (top row, with hat) was hired as head coach because he had played the sport at the University of Pennsylvania.*

points and touchdowns only four back then). In a return match four weeks later the Tide won 14-0, keyed by Grayson's 65-yard touchdown run. The team then finished its first season on February 22, 1893 – whether that was the last game of the 1892 season or the first of the 1893 season was debated for years thereafter – with a loss to intrastate rival Auburn, 32-22.

The Tide played its first intercollegiate rival, Sewanee, in 1893, and lost 20-0 as part of a dismal 0-4 season. The following year, they travelled to Jackson, Mississippi and in the first football game ever played in that city, lost to Ole Miss 6-0. But a week later, Alabama hit New Orleans and beat Tulane 18-6 as player-coach Abbott, also a running back, scored four times. That year also saw the formation of the Southern Intercollegiate Athletic Association, the ultimate forerunner of the Southeastern Conference. Even with a new organization,

the game was having its growing pains, particularly in financial areas. For example, Otto Wagonhurst coached Alabama in 1896 for a promised salary of $500. He got the first $50, and later another $50 after a special fund-raiser, but it wasn't until Alabama returned from its first Rose Bowl game in 1927 with a hefty check that they cleaned up their books, located Wagonhurst working for a rubber company in Akron, Ohio, and mailed him his check for the remaining $400.

The game also took its share of knocks in the board rooms. The school's board of trustees ruled after the 1896 season that no games could be played off campus, and the program nosedived. An increasing number of injuries in a violent sport which had come to rely more on massed formations than on finesse and all-around athletic skill led the board to go a step further by suspending football altogether for the 1898 season.

Right: *J. W. H. (Doc) Pollard, the first Alabama coach to win 20 football games, had a 21-4-5 record from 1906-09. His teams split a pair of games against Auburn before the series was broken off, and beat Tennessee four times.*

Right: *Derrill Pratt had never seen a football game when he played his first game for Alabama in 1907. He later played major league baseball.*

Far right: *W. T. (Bully) Vandegraaff was Alabama's first All-America player. He was a running back and lineman from 1912-15 and following graduation, enrolled at West Point and played for Army.*

Instability also reigned on the gridiron as coaches came and went for the next few years, sometimes in a comical manner. In the 1900 Auburn game, an Alabama supporter threw his hat into the air and Tide tackle M. H. Harvey kicked it for a mock field goal. The next year, he was the team's head coach. But the school has always marked a 36-0 victory over Georgia in 1904, the first year that it played a 10-game schedule, as a watershed: It was the team's 29th victory against 28 losses. The football program has been above .500 ever since, and as the last decade of the twentieth century began, it ranked fourth among all colleges in number of victories.

The program began to stabilize by 1906 when J. W. H. (Doc) Pollard was hired as head coach. He became the school's first "20-game winner," with a 21-4-5 record in 1906-09.

During that time, Alabama's foremost player was Derrill Pratt, a running back who played in the first game he ever saw after just three days of practice in 1907. He was a fine kicker, and the first Alabama graduate to play a major league sport, joining baseball's St. Louis Browns in 1912 and then the Yankees in 1918.

It wasn't until 1915 that Alabama finally had its first All-America player – W. T. (Bully) Vandegraaff, the third of three brothers from Tuscaloosa who were all four-year starters. Bully played tackle and fullback, and was the team's kicker, averaging 55 yards per punt during his career. In his senior season, 1915, he kicked 12 field goals and 26 of 28 extra points, including 19 in a row. His most memorable game occurred that year when Alabama beat Sewanee, then one of the South's most powerful teams, for the first time ever – his kicks accounted for 17 points, and he added a 78-yard punt. With the score tied in the fourth quarter, Vandegraaff rushed the Sewanee passer, knocked the ball out of his hands, caught it and romped 65 yards for a touchdown. He then kicked the extra point and also added two field goals in the 23-10 victory.

Though he weighed less than 150 pounds, Vandegraaff was the key player in coach Bibb Graves's "tackle around" play, scoring at least one touchdown in every game when he wasn't opening holes for other backs. In his senior season, he scored six TDs and played the equivalent of linebacker on defense, once returning a fumble 50 yards for a touchdown against Tennessee. He later coached at Alabama for Xen Scott and Wallace Wade, and had a fine career as football coach and athletic director at Colorado College.

When the 1920s began, Alabama football took a giant step forward when Charles Bernier became athletic director. He was a vigorous recruiter of athletic and coaching talent who had first hired coach Xen Scott and assistant coach Hank Crisp. It was Crisp who provided the "glue" that held the traditions of Alabama in place during a succession of coaches which spanned more than three decades at the University. He coached the line for 30 years under five coaches, spent 18 years as head basketball coach (with 266 wins), also coached baseball and track, and served two tours as athletic director – all this though he had lost his right hand at age 13 in a farming accident.

Bernier's early recruiting around the state of Alabama also brought such fine players as Riggs Stephenson and the Sewell brothers, Luke and Joe, to the University. All three later starred in major league

baseball. Luke Sewell managed the St. Louis Browns, winning the American League pennant in 1944. His brother Joe was a superlative hitter who was inducted into the Hall of Fame in 1976. Joe was graduated from the University in June 1920, and four months later was playing for the

Left: *Joe Sewell (seen here) and his brother Luke starred in football and baseball at Alabama. Joe is a member of major league baseball's Hall of Fame.*

Above: *D. V. (Bibb) Graves's 1911-14 teams, starring the Vandegraaff brothers, had a 21-12-3 record.*

Left: *Athletic director Charles Bernier brought great players and coaches to Alabama, helping to establish its great football legacy.*

Cleveland Indians in the World Series. He also returned to coach Alabama's baseball team. Stephenson, who University president Dr. George Denny once called "the embodiment of cleanliness, manliness and courage," played in two World Series while with Cleveland and the Chicago Cubs.

Xen Scott came to Alabama from Cleveland where he had played at Western Reserve University and then worked as a sportswriter covering horse racing for a Cleveland newspaper. He was the 15th head coach in 25 years at Alabama, but he brought some much needed stability to the program and paved the way for the great successes that followed after his departure in 1922. His first team in 1919, with Stephenson and Luke Sewell as its young stars, was unscored upon in its first five games and won eight of nine, while his 1920 team, with its 10-1 record, was the first Alabama team to win 10 games. One of these victories was 14-7 over Vanderbilt, the first time Alabama had beaten the Commodores after absorbing defeats by such scores as 78-0, 30-0, and 34-0. But the singular feat of that team was playing three games within a week. The Tide started by losing to Georgia 20-14, as the Bulldogs scored by recovering a fumble, blocking a field goal and returning another that was short. Four days later, on November 24, Alabama defeated

Mississippi State 24-7 as Stephenson completed 10 passes; and three days later, Alabama took its first trip north, blasting Case College 40-0 in Cleveland as Stephenson and Al Clemens each scored twice.

Scott's biggest achievement in his 29 victories over four seasons was a stunning 9-7 victory over mighty Pennsylvania in Philadelphia in 1922. The Tide were huge underdogs, with famed sportswriter Grantland Rice pronouncing that the game would give Penn a "breather." Eastern football was without peer – at least in the minds of those who played and coached it, and often in the minds of those who just knew about it. Scott knew he had to make his players believe that an eastern team was just as beatable as anyone else, so en route to Philadelphia by train, he stopped in Washington and took his team to see Navy defeat Penn State 14-0. His players realized that eastern teams were as vulnerable as any others, and that belief gave Scott the edge he sought.

Before a crowd of some 25,000 in Penn's Franklin Field, Alabama grabbed a 3-0 lead on Bull Wesley's 35-yard field goal, but Penn then took the lead on George Sullivan's 35-yard TD run. In the fourth quarter, Bill Bay set up the Tide's winning score with a 25-yard run to the four-yard line. Pooley Hubert carried to the goal line and fumbled the ball, but Short Probst pounced on it for the touchdown and an eventual 9-7 victory. This game became the turning point for Alabama football – it proved that the Tide could play and win against any team in the country.

Scott's final team then won three of its last four games and finished with a 6-3-1 record. But due to increasingly poor health, Scott had tendered his resignation a few weeks before the Penn game, and a short time after the season ended, he died.

One other major factor during this time helped build a solid foundation for Alabama football: Dr. George (Mike) Denny became University president in 1912. He was a superlative administrator, and one who believed that intercollegiate football was a rallying point for students and alumni. He also firmly believed that the sport was a means whereby his school's reputation and income could be enhanced by its success on the playing field. "The better the team, the larger the gate, the better the team," was his motto. He also let his coaches and athletic administrators know that he expected them to succeed, and he backed up that demand by promising them that they would have the talent to make it possible. He took an active interest in seeing that this was accomplished, spending many fall afternoons watching the team practice and never missing a game.

The physical monuments to his dedication to and interest in the sport on Alabama's campus followed when Denny Field was named in his honor in 1915; then came Denny Stadium in 1929, which continued to grow as Alabama football achieved new heights; and finally, Bryant-Denny Stadium was rededicated in 1976.

But physical monuments aside, perhaps the greatest legacy he left to Alabama's football program was his decision in 1923 to hire the first of its great coaches – Wallace Wade.

Below: Alabama president Dr. George (Mike) Denny gave total support to making a top-flight football program at Alabama.

Bottom: George Denny began construction of a stadium on Alabama's campus that later would bear his name.

2. The Tide Arrives

If Alabama's 9-7 upset victory over the University of Pennsylvania in 1922 is considered its first momentous football achievement, then the arrival of Wallace Wade as head coach in 1923 must be considered the most important factor in beginning its unparalleled record of success.

From 1923 through 1930, Wade brought Alabama into national prominence as a southern football powerhouse. His teams twice were named as national collegiate champions, and thrice reached the Rose Bowl, winning two games and tying another. Into the Tide's football history

Right: *Wallace Wade's coaching genius put Alabama among the nation's top college teams during his 1923-30 tenure. His teams won 61 games, including 20 in a row, and had two victories and a tie in three Rose Bowl appearances.*

during these years came such great players as Johnny Mack Brown, Herschel (Rosey) Caldwell, Pooley Hubert, Bill Buckler, and Hoyt (Wu) Winslett, all of whom helped the Tide to three unbeaten seasons in 1925, 1926, and 1930 while Wade was compiling a record of 61 victories, 13 losses, and three ties. During that time, Alabama had the second longest winning streak in its history – 20 games (from the last game of 1924 through the ninth game of the 1926 season), a mark which stood as the best for over a half century until Bear Bryant's 1978-80 teams reeled off 28 consecutive victories.

Wade's arrival at Alabama was the direct result of some bureaucratic bumbling by the University of Kentucky. Wade had spent two seasons as an assistant to Dan McGugin at Vanderbilt where the Commodores had gone unbeaten, and though wooed by both Kentucky and Alabama, Wade was ready to accept the job at Kentucky. After his interview in Lexington, Wade was asked to wait while the athletic committee met to make a decision. He sat for more than an hour in a hotel lobby, and just as the voting slips were being put into a hat by the committee, Wade angrily knocked on the meeting room door, strode in and told the committee what he thought of them and their job. He then finished his discourse by guaranteeing that no Kentucky team would ever beat one of his Alabama teams. With that, he strode out, called Tuscaloosa and told Alabama he was ready to take charge of their football team – and true to his word, he went on to win all eight games that his teams played against Kentucky.

A veteran of World War I combat in France, Wade carried his army drill sergeant techniques into his football, a stunning contrast to the easygoing Xen Scott. He was very discipline-oriented and tough on his players in what he expected of them. He was a "hands on" perfectionist as a coach, who drilled his players to perfect the most intricate hand and foot movements. He used a metronome to ensure proper timing, sometimes rehearsing a play for two months before using it. He even got down on the ground with a player, whether he was a first or third stringer, to demonstrate exactly what he wanted. Plays were rerun time after time if he saw something wrong, yet he did not dull his teams with long, arduous practices. This brought instant success as Alabama won seven games in 1923, lost only two (25-0 at Syracuse and 16-6 in the final game against Florida), and tied one (a scoreless game against Georgia Tech).

While Wade's coaching style finely honed his players, he also had inherited some fine

talent from Scott, including a young sophomore running back named Johnny Mack Brown, one of four brothers to play for the Tide. Brown was the centerpiece for the 1923-25 teams. He became known as the "Dothan Antelope," because the 180-pound native of Dothan, Alabama had a marvelous open-field style of running that many said resembled an antelope on the move. His career was storybook stuff during the Roaring Twenties when America loved storybook heroes, particularly dashing college football stars. There was not a faster running back in the country than Brown, and Wade even devised the first pair of "low cut" football shoes, in a time when everyone wore high tops, to help him add more speed.

Above: *Johnny Mack Brown was one of Hollywood's first great western movie stars, but from 1923-25 he was unsurpassed as a runner and pass receiver. He was Alabama's greatest all-around player to that time, and one of its best ever.*

He also was a fine pass receiver in an era when the pass was not used often except at Alabama, where the imaginative Wade mustered any weapon he believed would give his team more punch. Wade made the pass effective with such great personnel as Brown, end Rosey Caldwell, and fullback Pooley Hubert.

Brown's first football splash came in 1923 when he scored a touchdown in the Tide's 55-0 victory over Mississippi. In 1924, Alabama began its season auspiciously with a 55-0 pasting of Union in which Brown scored three times. Against favored Georgia Tech in Atlanta, he caught a 37-yard touchdown pass from Grant Gillis in a 14-0 upset victory. He had an 80-yard touchdown run on the game's first play in a 61-0 win against Mississippi. After a stunning 17-0 loss to Centre College that cost it an unbeaten season and a possible invitation to the Rose Bowl (there were no other post-season games at this time), Alabama was an underdog to once-beaten Georgia. Brown intercepted a pass and ran 65 yards for a touchdown to highlight a great defensive performance in a 33-0 victory. In fact, Wade's defense, keyed by Brown in the secondary and linemen Bruce Jones and Buckler, shut out its first six opponents in 1924.

That 1924 team, which won the school's first Southern Conference title (the conference encompassed every school in the South) also had fine overall talent. Wade often said that Gillis's punting skills were as important to his team's defensive play as to its overall ability because he kept opponents backed up throughout a game. Gillis and Hubert also were fine passers and Caldwell, an end, was the team's best receiver.

In 1925, Alabama finally won the jackpot by winning all ten of its games. "This was a team of experienced players, a great blocking team, and strong on defense," Wade later said. "It had a varied offense, using linebucking, open-field running, forward passing and kicking. It had excellent quarterbacking by Pooley Hubert, and used few substitutes.

"That team also earned its championship because it went through a hard schedule, was a high point-scorer and had only one touchdown scored on it during the regular season. It also made one of the great comebacks in Rose Bowl history, scoring three touchdowns in six minutes early in the second half."

Hubert and Brown were a deadly combination for the Tide in 1925. Wade used the single wing, the spread and short punt formations, and gave his backs a variety of tasks. Hubert played fullback, wingback, and tailback, while Brown, who was not a

good passer, played wingback and tailback where his running and pass-catching abilities were showcased. While Brown got so much of the notoriety, it was Hubert, who had come to Alabama as a tackle but was switched to fullback, and played linebacker on defense, who made many key plays. Against Georgia Tech, it was said that he made 25 tackles, and had similar figures in Alabama's victory over Washington in the Rose Bowl. His best day as a running back came against LSU in 1925 when he scored five touchdowns. He also passed to Winslett for the game's only touchdown against Mississippi A&M (now Mississippi State) and had another pair in a 34-0 victory over Florida. When the Tide finished its unbeaten season with a 27-0 win over Georgia, Hubert was part of a tricky triple TD pass to Gillis, and scored another touchdown. He was chosen the conference's most valuable player.

The biggest game of the 1925 season was Alabama's 7-0 victory over unbeaten Georgia Tech on a wet field in Atlanta. Brown scored the only touchdown on a twisting, 55-yard punt return during which Alabama blockers knocked down every Tech player – and the referee. Buckler threw the final block before Brown scored.

The Helms Athletic Foundation and Football Annual both named the Tide as national champion, the first of 11 titles the school has accumulated. For the first time ever, bowl talk was rampant in Tuscaloosa, but in a muddled sense because Colgate and Tulane also were being touted as foes against the Pacific Coast Conference champion Washington Huskies. Wade, in his usual blunt manner, didn't like the runaround and at first said that Alabama wasn't

Opposite: *Hoyt (Wu) Winslett (in dark jersey) was one of the star backs on Alabama's 1925 and 1926 national champion teams.*

Above: *Johnny Mack Brown led a 20-point, seven-minute third quarter explosion against Washington that sent Alabama to a 20-19 victory in their first Rose Bowl appearance in 1926.*

Overleaf: *Johnny Mack Brown finished his career at Alabama after the 1925 season, but the family tradition carried on as his brother Red Brown carried the ball against Stanford during a 7-7 tie in the 1927 Rose Bowl that capped a second straight national championship and an unbeaten season.*

Right: *Movie star Marion Davies was "mascot" for both Alabama and Stanford at the 1927 Rose Bowl. Alabama's Emile Barnes is on her right.*

interested in going to the Rose Bowl. But within days, the official invitation was offered and the Tide became the showcase for the South's wide-open brand of football.

It paid off, too, because after trailing 12-0 at the half, Hubert and Brown led a 20-point explosion in a seven-minute span of the third quarter that propelled the Tide to a 20-19 victory.

While many wondered whether Alabama's success in 1925 would be a one-time thing, Wade's team answered the doubters with another unbeaten season in 1926 — only a 7-7 tie against Pop Warner's Stanford team in the Rose Bowl spoiled a perfect season. Many believe this was Wade's best coaching job at Alabama, because graduation had stripped him of Brown and other fine backs. However, he had what Caldwell, who moved up from his role as understudy to Brown and was named to the All-Conference team as a running back, once called "a colorful cast of characters" in Emile (Lovely) Barnes, James (Goofy) Bowdoin, and Melvin (Snake) Vines. Alabama also featured a fine line plus a clever passing game to make up for lack of a rushing offense. One observer called it "a cold, calculating, and relentless outfit. Its blocking, tackling and precision in the execution of plays was outstanding."

Some season highlights: In a 19-7 victory over Vanderbilt and Wade's old boss, Dan McGugin, Red Brown, Johnny Mack's brother, set up one touchdown with a 58-yard run, and Wu Winslett threw a pair of TD passes to Caldwell. In the Tide's 21-0 victory over Georgia Tech, Winslett completed two of only four passes for touch-

downs. Against Mississippi A&M the Tide's defense intercepted seven passes and returned two for scores (many teams didn't even attempt that many passes in an entire game) and won 26-7. A blocked punt for a safety resulted in a 2-0 win over Sewanee, and Ben Enis returned two blocked punts for scores in a 24-0 win against LSU.

Once more, Pasadena and the Rose Bowl beckoned for a game against Stanford. This time the Tide came away with a 7-7 tie. And for the second straight season, the Helms Athletic Foundation picked Alabama as national champion.

It didn't take long for Alabama's fans to become spoiled — while Wade produced winning teams in the next three seasons, there were no bowl bids or conference titles, and a great deal of grumbling ensued. Turned off by what he considered crass ingratitude after a 6-3 season in 1929, Wade proceeded to sign a contract to become Duke's head coach after his contract with Alabama expired in 1930.

He went out with a flourish in leading the Tide to its third undefeated season and national championship and fourth conference title, as well as its second Rose Bowl victory. This team still is considered one of the greatest ever developed in the South — "exceptionally well-balanced . . . a good defensive team, and it had a good running attack, both through the line and in the open field," Wade said many years later. He had such fine players as linemen Fred Sington (an All-America tackle who is a member of Alabama's "All-Time" team), Frank Howard (later a distinguished head coach at Clemson), Jess Eberdt, and John Miller;

end Jimmy Moore; and backs John (Sugar) Cain and "Monk" Campbell.

Sington was the finest lineman of his time while at Alabama. Notre Dame coach Knute Rockne, whose Seven Mules offensive line was one of the most popular in the game's history, once called him "the greatest tackle in football history." Sington, an honor graduate, went on to play major league baseball for the old Washington Senators and Brooklyn Dodgers. He also starred in another role – as the honoree in singer Rudy Valee's top-rated 1930 hit, "Football Freddie:" "Football Freddie, rugged and tanned/Football Freddie, the All-America man."

With such players as "Football Freddie" Sington, Wade also had enough depth that he could start his "shock troops," or second team, in every game of the season – a tactic highly favored at that time to soften up the opposition before sending in the first team at the start of the second quarter. Though there was only minimal optimism for a championship season, the Tide rarely was pushed to win any of its nine scheduled games. The key win was a 13-0 victory over Georgia in the final game of the season, with the Rose Bowl bid on the line for each school, as Cain and Campbell took turns setting up each other's TDs with long runs. The Tide then stunned Washington State 24-0 with a fine passing attack in the Rose Bowl – even more satisfying for Wade, because he was a member of the Brown University team that had lost to the Cougars in the 1916 Rose Bowl game.

Wade took 35 players to Pasadena for his final game as Alabama's head coach, and every one of them played in the game. Afterward they hoisted Wade on their shoulders and carried him off the field, ending the first great chapter in Alabama football history.

Above left: *Fred Sington was a two-time All-America tackle in 1929-30 and is considered one of the greatest linemen in Alabama football history.*

Left: *Halfback Monk Campbell (seen here) teamed with John (Sugar) Cain to lead Alabama to a 10-0 record, a national championship, and a Rose Bowl victory in 1930.*

Left: *Monk Campbell carries the ball against Washington State in the 1931 Rose Bowl, during which he scored twice on runs of one and 43 yards and kicked three PATs in the Tide's 24-0 victory.*

3. The Frank Thomas Era

Below: *President Herbert Hoover (center, standing, holding hat) poses with the 1931 Alabama team during its post-season visit to Washington, where it played a three-way exhibition game against Georgetown, George Washington and Catholic universities.*

When Alabama travelled to Pasadena for the 1931 Rose Bowl game, the party included a recent assistant coach at the University of Georgia: Frank Thomas.

Thomas had already been selected to replace Wallace Wade, who was leaving to become head coach at Duke, and for the next 15 years there was not another coach who could have brought Alabama more football glory. He had been meticulously prepared for the job, first as a starting quarterback for Knute Rockne at Notre Dame in 1921 and 1922. Though many of Rockne's great players had fine coaching careers, Thomas was one of only a few who genuinely desired to pursue a lifetime coaching career. He even turned down an opportunity to work for his old coach after graduation to take a job at Georgia, where he felt he would have a better chance to forge his own reputation. He thus became the first Rockne disciple to spread his football gospel to the South, during two stints as an assistant with the Bulldogs and three years as head coach at the University of Chattanooga in Tennessee.

Wade personally recommended Thomas as his successor to University president Dr. George H. Denny, in full knowledge that someone special would have to carry on the tradition of success and excellence he himself had established at Alabama during his

Left: *Frank Thomas played for Knute Rockne at Notre Dame and carried The Rock's system to The Capstone, where his meticulous planning and teaching helped to win 115 games, 91 of them coming in a 13-season span from 1933-45.*

tenure. He also knew that Dr. Denny was a most demanding person, and had placed the highest priority on success on the gridiron. Thomas found that out for himself immediately when, after accepting the job in a meeting with the president, he was told, "Now that you have accepted our proposition, I will give you the benefit of my own views . . . It is my conviction that material is 90 per cent, coaching ability 10 per cent. I desire further to say that you will be provided with the 90 per cent and that you will be held to strict accounting for the remaining 10 per cent."

Dr. Denny need never have worried. In his 15 seasons as head coach, from 1931 until illness forced him to resign after the 1946 season, his teams won 115, lost 24, and tied 7. From 1933 through 1945, they were 91-17-7, the best record in college football

during that time. Those Tide teams forged three 14-game winning streaks and another of 13 games; twice Thomas saw his teams named national champion by one of the rating services; he had three unbeaten seasons in 1934, 1936, and 1945; and won three Southeastern Conference championships outright and shared a fourth. He produced 16 All-Americans, including two of Alabama's greatest all-around stars, Millard (Dixie) Howell and Harry Gilmer, as well as Don Hutson, one of the greatest ends in the game's history. Like those three players, he too was elected to the College Football Hall of Fame, his honor a very distinctive one as a member of the first group of coaches to be inducted which included Amos Alonzo Stagg, Pop Warner, and his old mentor, Rockne.

For all that, Alabama was the prime

beneficiary. Wade, another Hall of Fame coach, had given the school's football fortunes great visibility in the South as well as national recognition; Thomas made the Tide's Southern reputation ironclad, and gave it a national prominence not seen again until Bear Bryant, his former pupil, had been head coach for several years in the 1960s.

Thomas did it the old-fashioned way – he earned it, and made all of his teams pay the same price. He was a smallish man, at five feet, eight inches and about 160 pounds, but no one was tougher. He once scolded a young sophomore tackle named Bill Lee, later one of the school's greatest linemen, for loafing; as he concluded his tongue-lashing, Lee turned his back. This so infuriated Thomas that he seized the player by the shoulders and tried to haul himself up physically to Lee's chin level to continue his scolding. The young player was so terrified that he never again came close to a mediocre performance, and was a unanimous All-America choice in his senior year.

Thomas's first team was decimated by graduation losses, but he did things his own way, first by junking Wade's system and in-stalling the Notre Dame offense he had learned under Rockne. He was often uncompromising but always realistic as to what it took to turn out a winning team, and he was never afraid to pick talented assistants, encouraging them to contribute. Assistant coaches J. B. Whitworth and Red Drew later became Tide head coaches, and Thomas inspired Bear Bryant to forego professional football and begin his coaching career as his assistant.

Thomas, like Wade, was a meticulous planner; but unlike Wade and his mentor, Rockne, he was never flamboyant. Rather, he relied on surety and a sound plan to key his team's successes. A case in point: Thomas knew that Tulane built its offense around an unbalanced line with a fullback spinner play, so he set up a special assignment for the strong side defensive guard (teams played a six-man defensive line at that time). Alabama won five out of six games using this defense against Tulane.

On offense, his single wing teams, often featuring the Notre Dame Box, used a balanced line, and lived with a weak-side trap system that was the best in the South. Year in and year out, his team played clas-

Below: *With the help of a lead block by Millard (Dixie) Howell (57), John (Sugar) Cain starts a 72-yard touchdown run for Alabama's only score in a 6-0 victory over St. Mary's University in California in the final game of the 1932 season.*

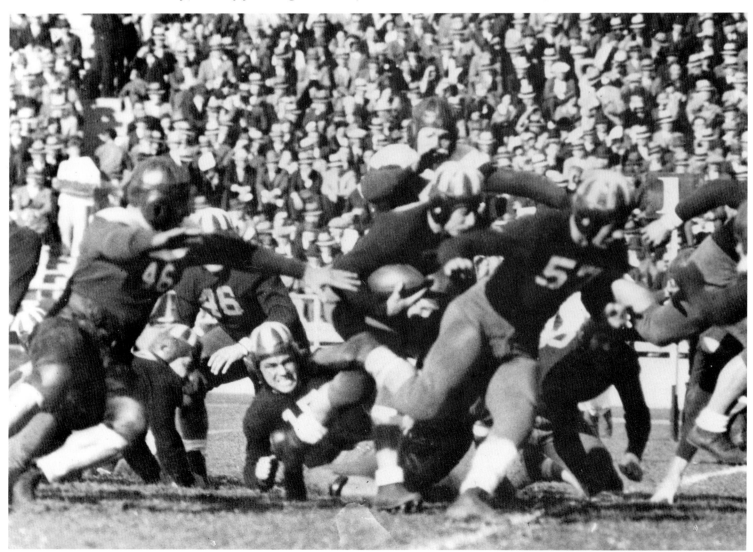

Left: *Coach Frank Thomas and one of his prize pupils, tackle Bill Lee, who was captain of the Tide's unbeaten 1934 national championship team that shut out five opponents and then beat Stanford's famed "Vow Boys" in the Rose Bowl.*

sic battles against Gen. Bob Neyland's Tennessee teams, which used strong-side traps and straight-ahead power. Inevitably, Thomas's special seven-man defensive line forced Neyland to abandon his bread-and-butter running game, and use a passing attack.

Just as important to Alabama's success under Thomas was his insistence on conditioning, a secret to his team's great late-season success and post-season record. Again, this was meticulously accomplished. His teams worked two-a-day sessions for the first two weeks of pre-season, the morning sessions in shorts and shirts, breaking twice for cool (never cold) water and sipping half-pints of orange juice when the session was finished. Then they took alternate tepid and cold showers. The afternoon sessions were always in full pads. At the halftime of each game, Thomas had his players remove their jerseys and shoulder pads and bathe from the waist up. The players always maintained that that simple procedure enabled them to win many games in the second half because they came out so refreshed.

All of this began in the 1931 season when,

despite graduation losses, his team lost only to Tennessee. The two teams staged another classic game in 1932, again won by Tennessee, but the punting duel between the Vols' Beattie Feathers and John (Sugar) Cain of Alabama still is considered one of the greatest in football history. The game was played on a muddy field in Birmingham and the teams preferred to punt on first or second down rather than to handle the slippery ball. Thus, Cain kicked the ball 19 times for a 48-yard average; Feathers punted 21 times for a 43-yard average. Ironically, after Feathers had killed a punt at Alabama's one-yard line in the third quarter, Cain's return kick from the end zone travelled just 12 yards and set up Feathers's touchdown that erased a 3-0 Alabama lead. Tennessee won 7-3.

Thomas soon discovered why Wade had decided to leave. Though Thomas had a 17-3 record in his first two seasons, he began to hear rumblings of discontent, particularly over his team's inability to defeat archrival Tennessee. Again, there were no post-season games other than the Rose Bowl to mollify the disenchanted, so Thomas had no opportunity to end his seasons with the

glories that bowl victories can bring.

However, he did find a "distraction" on his 1933 team with a young junior named Millard (Dixie) Howell. Howell had come from tiny Hartford, Alabama as an end, but his punting ability so caught Thomas's eye that he made him a back and designated him to replace Cain, who had graduated. He got his first action in an opening game, a 34-0 rout of Oglethorpe, and he so impressed Thomas that the coach moved him into the starting backfield where he gained 133 yards the next week in a scoreless tie against Mississippi. Thomas began to build some offense especially for Howell, and it paid off in an 18-0 win over Mississippi State.

Tennessee, the bane of Thomas's existence – and perhaps the key to holding his job – was next on the schedule. A Feathers touchdown gave Tennessee a 6-0 halftime lead, and the tension was so high that even the usually unflappable Thomas got caught up – when he stuck the lit of end of his cigar into his mouth during one play, he so broke up his players that they seemed to relax. In the third quarter, Howell so deftly executed a handoff that he was buried by Tennessee tacklers while Erskine Walker took the ball and ran for a touchdown. Howell then scored in the fourth quarter to give Alabama a 12-6 victory.

Thus began what really was an abbreviated career for a back who many still believe to be the finest all-around player in Alabama history. His level of perfection in running, passing, kicking, handling the ball, and playing defense has rarely been equalled, and no player has ever matched his all-around excellence. He only weighed 160 pounds, yet more than a half-century after he finished playing his name still dots the Alabama football record book. His 89-yard punt against Tennessee in 1933 is still the longest in the school's history; he ranks ninth in all-time rushing for a single season, with 840 yards in 124 carries in 1933, and is eleventh on the all-time career list with 1508 yards and an average of 6.3 yards per carry. In 1933, he rolled up a combined total of 1437 yards in nine games, and that still ranks twelfth in Alabama history; the next year, he added another 1157 yards.

Howell had the perfect partners in ends Don Hutson, who consistently ran the hundred yards in 9.8 seconds, and Paul "Bear" Bryant, who ran it in 10 seconds flat. With this trio, plus other stars such as fullback Joe Demyanovich, quarterback Riley Smith, halfback Jim Angelich, and Lee in the line, in 1933 Alabama had the first of 19 Southeastern Conference titles it has won or shared. It was unbeaten and won the national championship and the Rose Bowl in 1934 with a team that all agreed was even better and deeper than Wade's national championship team in 1930, which had been considered the best ever at Alabama up until that time.

Like Bryant, Hutson was a native of Arkansas. He had come to Alabama as a baseball player but decided to try football, and didn't spark any interest until midway through his junior season in 1933, when assistant coach Red Drew noticed that he "seemed to shuffle along but no one caught him." The turning point of the 1934 season came in a 13-6 victory over Tennessee when a Howell-to-Hutson pass set up Alabama's first touchdown and Hutson scored on one of

Opposite: *Halfback Dixie Howell ran, passed, kicked, and played defense better than anyone in Alabama history from 1932-34.*

Below: *Alabama's 1934 national champions: Linemen Bear Bryant, Bill Lee, Bob Morrow, Kavanaugh Francis, Charlie Marr, Jim Wahtley and Don Hutson; backs Jim Angelich, Joe Demyanovich, Riley Smith, and Dixie Howell.*

Above: *End Don Hutson was the star receiver for Alabama's 1934 national champions, but his greatest fame came in the NFL with the Green Bay Packers.*

Above right: *Riley Smith was quarterback of the Tide's 1934 national championship team.*

his famed end-around plays. Thomas then told his players they could go unbeaten, and they responded to the challenge for the rest of the season. Howell gained 153 yards in a 26-6 victory over Georgia; he and Riley used Hutson to roll up 170 passing yards in beating Kentucky 24-14; and together they all buried Clemson 40-0. In the final game of the season, against Vanderbilt, with a Rose Bowl bid on the line, Howell had his finest game of the season, rushing for 162 yards, adding 124 on punt returns, and punting for a 40-yard average. When Angelich broke into the clear on a 70-yard TD interception return to cap a 34-0 victory, Alabama's band broke out a lively rendition of "California, Here I Come!"

And to California they went, to play Stanford, led by its great fullback Bobby Grayson. The details of Alabama's 29-13 victory in the 1935 Rose Bowl are covered in Chapter 8.

Though Alabama went unbeaten again two years later in 1936 (the only blemish was a scoreless tie against Tennessee), it didn't get a post-season bid. Thomas was bitterly disappointed, because his ultimate aim at the start of every season was to produce a record good enough to get his team invited for post-season play, and he couldn't understand how the Rose, Sugar, Orange, and Sun bowls could pass up an unbeaten

team. Thomas used this snub as a club to drive his 1937 team back to Pasadena with an unbeaten season that really was a reward for overachievement, because his team struggled for every victory. Alabama had to play mistake-free football to win, and when it committed eight turnovers against California in the Rose Bowl, the Tide lost 13-0.

Thomas had some new stars though, including running backs Herkey Moseley and Joe Kilgrow, a 180-pound All-American from Montgomery, who also was a star third baseman on the baseball team; tackle Jim Ryba; and a pair of great guards, Leroy Monsky, a 215-pound All-America selection in 1938, and Arthur (Tarzan) White, a 210-pounder who was a three-year starter, earned Phi Beta Kappa honors and later earned a doctorate from Columbia University while also wrestling professionally and playing for the NFL's New York Giants.

Once more Thomas began to hear alumni grumbling, despite a 19-6-2 record from 1938 through 1940, beginning with 7-1-1 in 1938 that included an upset 19-7 victory over Southern California in Los Angeles in the first game of the season. His "worst" (5-3-1) season at Alabama was in 1939 when he did not have any talent at quarterback, but the Tide still upset a great Fordham

Left: *Tailback Joe Kilgrow was a star for Frank Thomas, leading Alabama to a perfect season in 1936, two SEC titles in 1936-37, and a trip to the 1938 Rose Bowl.*

Below: *Kilgrow (dark jersey, with ball) sets up the game-winning field goal in a 9-7 victory over Vanderbilt that clinched a trip to the 1938 Rose Bowl.*

Right: *Bobby Jenkins goes up and over against Boston College during Alabama's 37-21 come-from-behind win over Boston College in the 1943 Orange Bowl. Jenkins scored twice in Alabama's first trip to that post-season game.*

team 7-6 in New York City. His best player in those seasons was Charley Boswell, later one of America's most courageous athletes when he shrugged off blindness caused by battle wounds in World War II and became the nation's foremost blind golfer for several decades.

In 1941, Thomas once again had a national championship with a team that was rich in talented backs – Jimmy Nelson, Billy Harrell, Julius Papas, Sumpter Blackman, Paul Spencer, Al Sabo, Vaughn Tollett, Carl Mims, Howard Hughes, Bart Avery, Ross Moseley, Louis Scales, Dave Brown, George Gammon, and Russ Craft. Thomas sent them in waves at opponents, and won eight of ten games. Alabama then rolled over Texas A&M 29-21 in the Cotton Bowl.

There were two key games during that season: a 19-14 victory over Tulane that was decided in the final minute, and a great defensive effort in which the Tide stopped Georgia's great All-America back Frank Sinkwich in a 27-13 victory. In the Tulane game, Alabama trailed the Green Wave 14-13 in the final minutes when Nelson quick-kicked 66 yards to Tulane's 12-yard line. The Wave then kicked out to its 40, and seven plays later, with less than a

minute to play, Don Salls scored the winning touchdown.

In 1942, with such players as Joe Demyanovich and tackle Don Whitmire, later a great All-America player and Hall of Famer at the Naval Academy and a famed Navy admiral, Alabama forged a 7-2 record and got a trip to the Orange Bowl. In a key 8-0 victory over Tennessee, Bobby Jack Jenkins ran 34 yards on a spinner play for the only touchdown. He duplicated the feat for 40 yards against Boston College in the bowl game.

World War II had intervened and Alabama dropped the sport in 1943, but resumed it the following year with Thomas's famed "War Babies," a group of freshmen and 4-F students who either were ineligible for military service or awaited a callup. The star of this group, and a player of nearly equal magnitude to Dixie Howell, was Harry Gilmer, who carried Thomas's last few teams to the final bit of glory that he enjoyed at Alabama.

Gilmer was a slightly built back, weighing only 158 pounds, but he had big, strong hands and a durability that belied his slight frame. Thomas and many others at that time considered him one of the finest passers in college football history. He was also a great all-around back who was an excellent runner, kicker, and defensive player at a time when players went both ways – and great players like him were true triple threat stars. "I never saw anyone who knew so well what to do under all conditions," Thomas later said of his young star. "I never recall him throwing a bad or wild pass."

The 1944 team, composed nearly entirely of teenagers, won five of eight games, plus a tie, and upset unbeaten Mississippi State 19-0 en route to a Sugar Bowl date against Duke. The Tide, with Gilmer throwing three touchdown passes, led for most of that game before bowing in the final minutes.

In 1945, Gilmer took Thomas and the Tide to its last Rose Bowl. That season he completed nearly 69 percent of his passes and averaged more than 10 yards each time he ran the ball as he accumulated 1457 yards, eleventh best in a single season in Alabama history. He still ranks fifth among the school's passers with a career total of 2863 yards, including a total of 26 touchdowns.

When Thomas surrounded Gilmer with some great players, including All-America center Vaughan Mancha and fullback Lowell Tew, he had what most consider his greatest team – one that produced the school's first perfect record since 1934 and outscored opponents by an average 43-8 over the 10-game season, including a 34-14 romp against Southern Cal in the 1946 Rose Bowl. The team, though it still used the ancient Notre Dame Box formation, had dazzling speed to complement its well-balanced offense, one that was ranked second nationally while its defense was ranked first among all college teams. The highlight of its regular season was a 28-14 victory over Georgia, led by All-American Charlie Trippi. Gilmer, en route to All-America honors, threw three touchdown passes and finished the season as the SEC's most valuable player, beating out Trippi for that honor.

All of this success had exacted a vicious physical toll on Thomas, leaving him with a heart condition and high blood pressure, and throughout the 1945 season he complained of being constantly tired. As the 1946 season began and his health did not improve, he either spent his time in bed or working from a desk in a specially rigged trailer next to the team's practice field, because his doctors would not allow him to stand for long periods of time. His "War Babies," then mostly juniors, were joined by some veterans from earlier teams who had been in the service, but even with Gilmer having another fine season, Thomas's own spark was missing. The team won

Left: *Harry Gilmer rivaled Dixie Howell as Alabama's most prolific offensive player.*

Below: *Gilmer (No. 52) on one of 11 carries that netted him 116 yards and a TD in the Tide's 34-14 win over Southern California in the 1946 Rose Bowl.*

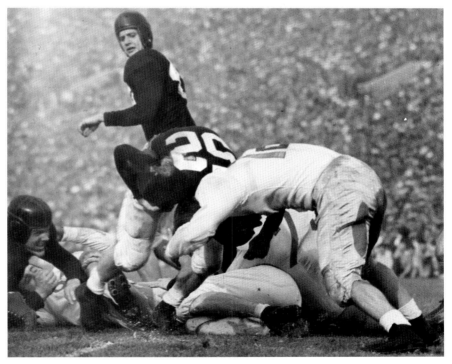

seven of its 11 games, and after winning its first four, he resisted a suggestion from University president Dr. Raymond Paty that he resign for his own good, a decision he later termed "foolish." He resigned at the end of the season and continued at Alabama as athletic director through 1951, when continued ill health finally took its toll. He passed away in 1954 at the relatively young age of 56, but he had long since established Alabama as one of college football's great powers and set a standard of excellence that only one other man – Bear Bryant – has matched.

4. Troubled Times

By 1947, Alabama's football fans were spoiled. For nearly a quarter-century, the Tide's football teams had been led by two of the best coaches in college football history. Such success has a way of anesthetizing reality for fans, who believed that Alabama could simply go out and hire a coach who would automatically be as good as Wallace Wade and Frank Thomas had been. But football programs simply don't work that way – not at Notre Dame, or Ohio State, or Southern Cal, or anyplace else, including Alabama. Harold (Red) Drew tried to take up the torch, and so did J. B. Whitworth, but for many of the years from 1947 through 1957 the down cycle that inevitably hits every football program served up great portions of humble pie at Alabama.

There were some good times, beginning with Drew's first season in 1947 when the team won eight of its 10 regular season games behind Harry Gilmer, but lost in the Sugar Bowl to Bobby Layne and the Texas Longhorns, 28-7. Thomas's "War Babies" had grown up to be seniors when Drew succeeded Thomas, under whom he had served as end coach for 11 years.

College football suddenly teemed with players who had either interrupted their careers or had postponed their start for military service in World War II, and competition was more balanced than ever. The edge that Alabama had enjoyed disappeared when its opponents had just as many good players.

At first, Alabama's fortunes gave no

Right: In 1948, Alabama and Auburn resumed a rivalry that had been terminated since 1907, and the Crimson Tide rolled to a 55-0 victory.

signs of sliding when Drew's 1947 team went to the Sugar Bowl, only to see Gilmer have the worst day of his career – and in his final game. He completed just three of 11 passes and gained just five yards rushing against the Longhorns. In 1948 and 1949, Alabama had trouble getting started, twice losing to Tulane and not being able to beat Vanderbilt in 1-2-1 starts. Auburn rejoined the schedule in 1948 after 41 years of silliness and petty squabbling with Alabama had kept the two natural rivals apart. The dispute was decided by legislative mandate, and the student body presidents of the two schools, Willie Johns of Alabama and

Gillis Cammack of Auburn, buried a hatchet in a hole in Woodrow Wilson Park in Birmingham. Alabama then went out and buried its rivals with a rousing 55-0 victory. (The Alabama-Auburn rivalry is covered in Chapter 7.)

During the 1948 and 1949 seasons, Alabama rooters continually sought another Harry Gilmer-type player, and most of their prayers were answered when Bobby Marlow, a young sophomore from Troy, Alabama, became the team's starting halfback. For the next three seasons, Marlow ran the football even better than Johnny Mack Brown, Dixie Howell, and Gilmer. In fact, only Johnny Musso and Bobby Humphrey in the four decades since Marlow played for the Tide have even come close to matching his feats, and during the decade of the 1950s no SEC back, including Heisman Trophy winner Billy Cannon at LSU, came close to matching his three-year rushing total of 2560 yards.

A measure of a player's greatness is his longevity on the statistics charts, and since the game has changed so radically since 1950 to include more games, anyone from that era and beyond who still is listed among the top statistical leaders was an extraordinary player. Marlow fits the bill,

because those 2560 yards in 34 games over three seasons rank third on Alabama's career rushing charts. (Humphrey ranks first with 3420 in 49 games, over four seasons.) Marlow's greatness is measured by his top ranked 6.3 yard average per carry in his varsity career, during which he also accumulated nine games of 100 or more yards. That, too, is an extraordinary figure for those years because 100-yard rushing games were platinum benchmarks, often achieved less than a dozen times in an entire season in all of college football.

Marlow had few peers among sophomore running backs anyplace in the nation in

Right: *Fullback Tommy Lewis was a three-season starter for the Tide in 1952-54 and coach Red Drew called him the best fullback he ever coached.*

1950 when he accumulated five of his 100-yard games, including his second all-time best of 180 yards against Georgia Tech in the ninth game of the year. The following week, he had 100 against Florida, and the week after closed the year with 113 against Auburn. He finished the season with 728 yards, for a 7.45 yards per carry average, which still ranks second in Alabama football history. He also scored four touchdowns in a 24-point performance against Georgia Tech, a figure which only Johnny Musso (1971) and David Casteal (1988) have matched.

In 1951, when Alabama had its first losing season (5-6) since 1900 (2-3), Marlow ripped off 233 yards in one game, second best in the history of Alabama football, against Auburn. Earlier in the year, he had 103 against Delta State, and he finished the year with 882 yards, still among the top 17 season performances by any Alabama running back.

Marlow had more help from Bobby Luna and Corky Tharp in 1952, but still had a career-high 950 yards that season, including 174 against Virginia Tech for a 11.6 yards per carry average, which ranks third in Tide history. Marlow also holds the Number 2 mark with 13.8 in his 180-yard

performance against Georgia Tech in 1950.

Marlow was still the bread-and-butter guy for Alabama in 1952, but Tharp was just warming up for a sensational three seasons during which he also helped Alabama to a pair of bowl games. He started the 1952 season as Marlow's sub but played so brilliantly that Drew moved Marlow to right halfback and installed Tharp as the regular left halfback. Luna, a four-year player from 1951 through 1954, backed up both players, and Drew added sophomore Tommy Lewis, who he called the best fullback he ever coached. Clell Hobson was quarterback of the 1952 team, backed up by a youngster from Montgomery named Bart Starr, who would somehow be a part of some of the most disappointing moments in Alabama football history and yet go on to stardom in the NFL with Green Bay.

Drew had one of his best teams in 1952. It won its first four games, fell apart against Tennessee, and then was superb for the rest of the season, except for a tough loss against Georgia Tech on national television. Tech ranked second nationally when it played Alabama, and quickly fell behind on Luna's first-quarter field goal. Georgia Tech scored the winning touchdown in the second quarter and then had to stop three big Ala-

Above: *Alabama crushed Syracuse 61-6 in the 1953 Orange Bowl with a 586-yard offensive performance that was keyed by its power-packed backfield of, from left, Bobby Marlow, Tommy Lewis, Clell Hobson, and Bobby Luna. Hobson threw a pair of TD passes and Luna and Lewis each scored twice.*

bama drives to gain a 7-3 victory. The following week, Alabama hit its peak with a rousing 27-7 victory over Maryland, a week after the Terps' two-year winning streak had been broken by Mississippi. Alabama's pass rush simply overwhelmed Maryland's All-America quarterback Jack Scarbath. The Tide closed the season with a 21-0 victory over Auburn and then accepted a date to play Syracuse, which had had its best season in a quarter-century, in the Orange Bowl.

January 1, 1953 was a landmark day in Alabama history as well as in college football history. No bowl team is ever nine touchdowns better than the other, but late in the third quarter, thousands were streaming from the Orange Bowl when Alabama's lead reached 41-6 en route to an eventual 61-6 victory over Syracuse. Also for the first time ever, the Rose, Sugar, Cotton, and Orange bowls all were televised nationally, and the thousands leaving the Orange Bowl were hurrying home to see the other games. At one point in the fourth quarter, an Orange Bowl committeeman approached the game's timekeeper and suggested that he keep the clock running so that the game, then running nearly three hours, would not be cut off from television before its conclusion.

Hobson passed for a pair of touchdowns to Luna and Tharp while Lewis added a pair, including a 30-yard run. Luna also ran 38 yards for a second TD and Tharp had a 12-yard run for his second TD. Hootie Ingram returned a punt for 80 yards and a TD and Buster Hill sped 60 with an intercepted pass. Even Starr got into the act, passing 22 yards to Joe Cummings for a TD as Alabama's passing game rolled up 300 yards, and it rushed for 286 more. "We didn't want to leave one record standing," tackle Van Marcus said.

Still, Alabama led 7-6 at the end of the first quarter and only 20-6 at the half, but then exploded for two 20-point quarters. "It was just one of those things that happened," Drew said later. "I just couldn't stop them. We didn't try to run up the score. Everybody just figured we had a particularly good football team on that day."

With Marlow gone in 1953, Lewis, Tharp, and Luna became the offensive stars. Tharp was worth the price of admission. He had astounded everyone in 1952 with an 83-yard run against Virginia Tech as part of a 163-yard rushing day; he scored on an 86-yard punt return against Georgia in 1953 while also gaining 100 yards rushing; and in 1954, he returned an interception 96 yards, longest in Alabama history, against Tennessee. His play helped the Tide to a 6-3-3 record in 1953, and overcame a stunning 25-19 opening game loss by Mississippi Southern. There were 7-7 ties against LSU and Mississippi State and a scoreless deadlock against Tennessee, but still the Cotton Bowl believed the Tide to be a worthy opponent against Rice.

There have been many memorable moments in Alabama's bowl history, but none has ever matched what happened in the 1954 Cotton Bowl when Tommy Lewis

Opposite: *Tommy Lewis (center, white helmet) scores his second TD in the 1953 Orange Bowl.*

Left: *Hootie Ingram (20), a future Alabama athletic director, breaks up a Syracuse pass.*

jumped off the Alabama bench to tackle Rice's Dickie Moegle as he sped past the Tide's bench en route to an apparent touchdown. That play (covered in Chapter 8) ranks with Roy Riegels's wrong-way run in the Rose Bowl as one of the most famous in college football bowl history.

Alabama lost that game 28-6, and it seems that that one bizarre moment triggered the gods of misfortune because Alabama then entered the bleakest period of its football existence. The Tide had four consecutive losing seasons, including 0-10 in 1955, and once went 20 consecutive games without a victory. Drew resigned after a 4-5-2 season in 1954, becoming a professor of physical education and fulltime track coach. He was succeeded by Whitworth, who also had been an assistant coach under Thomas and head coach at Oklahoma State. He lasted just three seasons.

Of course, everyone wanted to know why a program that had been so great for so long could take such a downward plunge. Part of the reason was the changes in the game itself, a move from two platoon to one platoon in 1953, and then the inability to attract good players and top flight coaches. There never was a lack of effort, and no one felt a keener disappointment than Drew and Whitworth as they failed to keep the Tide alive.

But help was on the way. The Bear was coming home.

5. The Bear

"We have secured . . . the best football coach in the country for the position of head football coach at the University of Alabama."

In that terse sentence, Paul William "Bear" Bryant was anointed as head coach at Alabama shortly after the end of the dismal 1957 season, and with his coming, the Crimson Tide rode a wave of popularity and success that its football program had never before enjoyed – and that's saying something, because both Wallace Wade and Frank Thomas had brought it some tremendous moments, and given it a well-deserved national reputation.

Bryant was already a legend of sorts when he came to Alabama – you don't have a nickname "Bear" without having done something to earn it – and he continued to build it for 25 seasons even as his teams

Right: *Paul (Bear) Bryant, 6'2" and 196 pounds, was an Arkansas native known as "the other end" on Alabama's 1934 national championship team that featured All-America receiver Don Hutson. He was an assistant coach at his alma mater for several seasons, and was named head coach in 1958.*

won six national championships; won out-right or shared 13 Southeastern Conference championships; and had three perfect seasons, ten others in which they lost just once, and another six when they only lost twice. Bryant never had a losing season during his quarter-century at Alabama, and he put together the school's longest winning streak ever, 28 games from the last nine games of the 1978 season through the seventh game of 1980, when he was already at an age when the whispers had become louder that he had "lost his touch." He fashioned other winning streaks, of 19 (all of 1961 through the eighth game of 1962); 17 (the final six games of 1965 through the entire 1966 season, plus the Sugar Bowl); two 12-game winning streaks; and four 11-game streaks. He also took his teams to 24 consecutive bowl games, for a 13-10-1 record, starting with the newly formed Liberty Bowl in Philadelphia in 1959 and ending with that same bowl, in Memphis, Tennessee in 1982. His final victory in his final game as head coach, in the 1982 Liberty Bowl, gave him 232 victories at Alabama, easily the most in the school's history and a major portion of his then all-time record 323 career wins.

Bryant, a native of Arkansas, had become an adopted son of Alabama during his playing days in the mid-1930s when he was a member of Frank Thomas's great teams that featured Dixie Howell and end Don Hutson. Bryant loved the "aw shucks" approach about his being "the other end," which many who played with him pooh-poohed because they said he was almost as good as Hutson.

He had achieved his own niche in football because he was forever fearful of returning to the poverty of his youth, during which, for a five dollar prize, he once agreed to wrestle a live bear at a carnival. Knowing enough to stay away from the animal's grasp and his razor-sharp claws, Bryant tumbled the bear to the ground and held on until the time expired, but never got his money because the promoter ruled it "no match." It cost him a nip of skin as the animal got in its last licks, and a lifetime nickname which became as much reality as legend because Bryant was an absolute "bear" whenever he drilled his football teams at Maryland, Kentucky, and Texas A&M before coming to Alabama. He had already won 91 games at those schools, taking two from oblivion to championship and post-season game honors.

Bryant was never a coach who believed in frills or fancy formations. In fact, his greatest strength lay in establishing rock-solid defenses and playing very basic offense. In the 1951 Sugar Bowl, his defense at Ken-

Left: *Bear Bryant had been head coach at Maryland, Kentucky, and Texas A&M before returning to his alma mater. When he retired after the 1982 season, he had won 325 games, more than any coach in history to that time.*

tucky shut down Bud Wilkinson's "unstoppable" Split-T offense that had averaged five and six touchdowns a game, breaking the Sooners' 31-game unbeaten streak. Wilkinson was so impressed that he took some of Bryant's defensive theories in exchange for some "inside" on his own offense. Wilkinson got the best of that deal because he took Bryant's principles and fashioned the "Oklahoma," or 3-4, defense that is still extensively used.

Yet Bryant never was stubborn to the point of ignoring change if it fit his personnel. For example, throughout the 1960s his offenses, with such quarterbacks as Pat Trammell, Joe Namath, Steve Sloan, Ken Stabler, and Scott Hunter, had featured some fine passing. But with the advent of the Wishbone offense in the early 1970s, Bryant found his newer quarterbacks more suited to the "bone." So he scrapped the balance of pass-to-run, and went to the Wishbone – but added his own touch by hooking on a passing capability that Wishbone offenses at such powers as Texas, Oklahoma, and Arkansas did not possess. Thus, Bryant always felt he had more than just one way to beat an opponent, and had a fallback weapon if he needed to catch up late in a game when time was precious.

In 1958, though, Bryant had just one thought in mind – to restore Alabama football to the pinnacles he had known as player and assistant coach some two decades before. "The reason, the only reason, I'm going back is because my school called me," Bryant said before leaving Texas A&M, where he was famous for taking two busloads of players to his first

Above: *Bear Bryant immediately energized Alabama's offense with a wide open passing game featuring Bobby Skelton passing to players such as end Bill Rice (85).*

"training camp" and having only half a busload return as members of the varsity.

His hard-edged approach to Alabama's football program was the same. He recognized that there were many good players, but felt that they had not been forced to work hard enough to perform to their full potential. All of that changed in 1958, Bryant's first year, as he turned out Alabama's first winning team in six years with a 5-4-1 record.

Bryant's first season is memorable because Alabama opened that season against eventual national champion Louisiana State University at Mobile, Alabama. While most of the LSU players considered the opener against the Tide a "breather," head coach Paul Dietzel and assistant Charlie McClendon both had worked for Bryant and knew their team was in for the fight of its life. Though LSU won 13-3, they had a stiff taste of Bryant's defensive genius, because they trailed 3-0 until early in the third quarter before their great talent, led by Heisman Trophy winner Billy Cannon, bailed out the win. Bryant gave them everything in his book, including a pair of quick kicks by Marlin Dyess that died at the seven- and six-yard lines. LSU's players later admitted the game was one of the toughest they had played that year and jerked them into the right frame of mind so that they would

never again suffer a letdown.

Bryant got his first SEC victory a few weeks later with a 9-7 triumph over Mississippi State when Fred Sington, son of the great Alabama tackle, kicked a 22-yard field goal and quarterback Bobby Jackson tossed a 21-yard TD pass to Norbie Ronsonet. He got his 100th victory the following season with a 19-7 win over Tulane with junior Bobby Skelton in his first start, as part of a nine-game unbeaten string (there were a couple of ties) that brought his first bowl invitation, to Bud Dudley's inaugural Liberty Bowl game. There he lost 7-0, when Penn State came up with a fake field goal play at the end of the first half in which the Nittany Lions' holder Galen Hall rolled to his right and passed to Roger Kochman for the game's only touchdown.

Bryant, of course, was bitterly disappointed – losing any game never was palatable to him, regardless of how well his team played or how much stronger the opposition – but it was apparent that he had Alabama headed back toward the top, because the team had won almost as many games in his first two seasons as in the previous five.

Bryant entered the 1960s with the first of his great quarterback brigade as Skelton and Pat Trammell divided the duties in 1960. Skelton was a skilled passer, and Trammell had better running ability and extraordinary leadership, which he displayed to the fullest the following season when the Tide went unbeaten and won its first national championship under Bryant.

In 1960, Alabama trailed Georgia Tech 15-0 before Trammell led the Tide to its first score. A leg injury forced him from the game, and Skelton came on and steered an 82-yard TD drive, then brought the Tide back for Richard O'Dell's game-winning 24-yard field goal with no time on the clock. The victory over Tech and its coach Bobby Dodd was particularly satisfying for Bryant, who preferred beating Dodd to any other rival. Dodd was just about the opposite of Bryant in his coaching style, and often won with what Bryant derisively referred to as "Dodd's Luck" because the Tech coach was renowned for coming up with game-winning plays when it seemed his team was destined to lose. Bryant, on the other hand, was always proud of the hard work and discipline that produced his team's success. This personal rivalry soon filtered down to the players, and then to the fans – the Tech fans often pelted Alabama's players with all sorts of flying missiles, including bottles, when the game was played at Grant Field in Atlanta. In fact, Bryant came onto the field for the final game in the series there in 1964 wearing a football helmet, which he claimed he needed for protection.

Georgia Tech was a 10-0 victim in Alabama's national championship season in 1961, part of a streak during which the Tide shut out its last five regular season opponents and allowed just 25 points in all, the fewest by any Bryant-coached team. This team had great leadership from Trammell, as well as fine players in running back Mike Fracchia, end Butch Wilson, and tackle Billy Neighbors. Trammell's high point that year came in a rollicking 34-3 victory over Tennessee, the first over the Vols since 1954. The win also gave the Tide some measure of revenge, because Tennessee had been the only team to beat them in 1960. Alabama clinched its national championship with a season-ending 34-0 romp of Auburn (the final polls were tabulated before the bowl games at that time). Trammell passed for one TD, scored another and watched as the Tide's top-ranked defense, led by All-America linebacker Leroy Jordan, never let Auburn past the 26-yard line. They capped the year by beating Arkansas 10-3 in the Sugar Bowl, the first perfect season for any Alabama team since Frank Thomas's 1945 team led by Harry Gilmer was 10-0.

Trammell departed from the Capstone after that season but Joe Namath, a slope-shouldered, black-haired youth from Beaver Falls, Pennsylvania had already

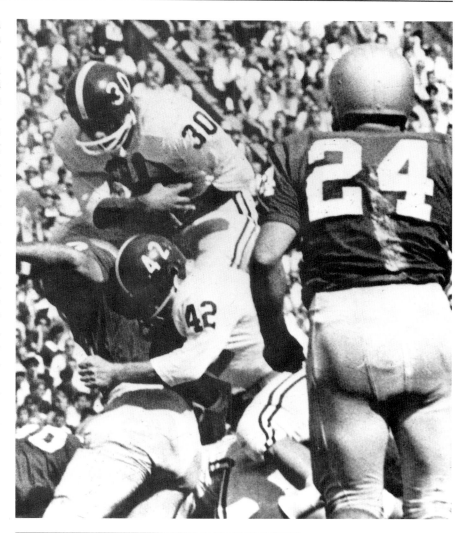

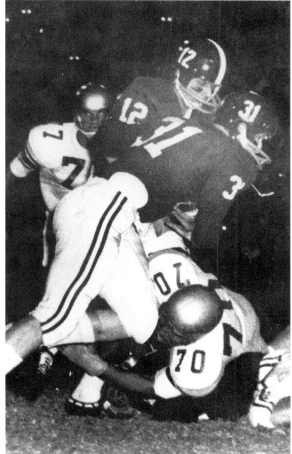

Above: *Mike Fracchia's TD helped the Tide defeat Georgia 32-6 in the opener of its 1961 national championship season.*

Left: *Joe Namath (12, dark helmet) directed Alabama to a 10-1 season as a sophomore in 1962.*

Right: *Coach Bryant is carried off the field after Alabama beat Mississippi 12-7 in the 1964 Sugar Bowl.*

Above: *Bryant called Joe Namath "the best athlete I've ever seen." In his senior year, with the help of Steve Sloan, Namath led the Tide to a national championship.*

Above right: *Bryant with QB Steve Sloan after winning the 1966 Orange Bowl and another national championship.*

shuffled onto the scene. In 1962 he began a three-year run during which he led Alabama to the 1964 national title (despite a 21-17 loss to Texas in the Orange Bowl) and accumulated an outstanding record before signing a world-class, $427,000 contract with the New York Jets.

Bryant called Namath "the best athlete I've ever seen . . . blessed with that rare quickness – hands, feet, everything . . ." Namath took the 1962 team to a 10-1 season, including a superb 17-0 victory over Oklahoma in the Orange Bowl. He had thrown a 52-yard touchdown pass to Richard Williamson on the fifth play of his first start in the opener against Georgia, a game that later became infamous as the focal point of a false charge that Bryant and Bulldogs athletic director and ex-coach Wally Butts had conspired to "fix" the game. The story appeared in the *Saturday Evening Post* magazine, and both men sued the publication for libel and won, collecting huge settlements that were key factors in the magazine's eventual demise. Namath ended the season as he had started – throwing a TD pass to Williamson, in the Orange Bowl victory.

The following season, Namath had the Tide moving strongly again but he also crossed paths with Bryant when he broke a team rule against drinking. He admitted the infraction before the team was to play its final regular season game against the University of Miami on national television, with a date against Mississippi also set for the Sugar Bowl. A Bryant rule was inviolable, and Namath was suspended for those

final two games. On came quarterbacks Jack Hurlbut and Steve Sloan and somehow the Tide won both, though even Bryant was surprised. "But after I got to thinking about it," he said later, "I said, 'Shoot, you can do anything if you want to bad enough.'"

The Namathless victories didn't come easily. It took a 102-yard opening kickoff return by Gary Martin and a pair of fumble recoveries that led to 10 more points, plus a last-ditch defensive stand that was keyed by Jackie Sherrill's final interception, to get a 17-12 win over Miami. In the Sugar Bowl, Tim Davis kicked a record four field goals for a 12-0 lead going into the last quarter. After Mississippi got its only touchdown to close the score to 12-7, Alabama's defense stopped the Rebels three times inside the 10-yard line.

Namath responded to Bryant's discipline by leading the Tide to victories in the first three games in 1964 before injuring his knee. Sloan came on to keep the string going and when Namath was healthy again, the pair split the job for the rest of the season, with Sloan coming on to pass in long-yardage situations because Namath was not very mobile. In the season finale against Auburn on Thanksgiving Day, Ray Ogden's 107-yard kickoff return keyed a 21-14 victory. Three days later, then top-ranked Notre Dame was upset by Southern Cal and Alabama became the nation's top-ranked team for the second time since Bryant had become head coach.

They were Number 1 again in 1965 as Sloan, along with receivers Dennis Homan and future Alabama coach Ray Perkins, led the Tide to a 9-1-1 record that was climaxed by a stunning 39-28 victory over Nebraska in the Orange Bowl. Alabama was stunned by Georgia in the season's first game when the Bulldogs, helped by a disputed "hook-and-ladder" pass-catch-and-lateral play, nipped the Tide 18-17 – but that would be the only loss of the season. Sloan led them to a 17-16 victory over Mississippi in the final seven minutes of the last quarter, running nine yards for the last touchdown. Three weeks later, Sloan hit Homan on a 65-yard TD pass, David Ray kicked a 27-yard field goal and the defense then held off Mississippi State in a 10-7 win.

Alabama was ranked fourth on New Year's Day morning but, when the day ended, the three teams in front of them – Michigan State, Arkansas, and Nebraska – all had lost and Alabama was crowned national champion, thanks to its win over the Huskers.

Bryant called his 1966 team "my uncrowned champions" because it won all of its 11 games but was ranked only third nationally. He considered it an even better

Left: *Bryant and his famed left-handed quarterback, Ken Stabler.*

Below: *Ken (The Snake) Stabler in action against Nebraska in the 1967 Sugar Bowl.*

Overleaf: *Hard-hitting defense, which caused opponents to fumble, was the hallmark of Bryant's teams, as in this game against Mississippi in 1967.*

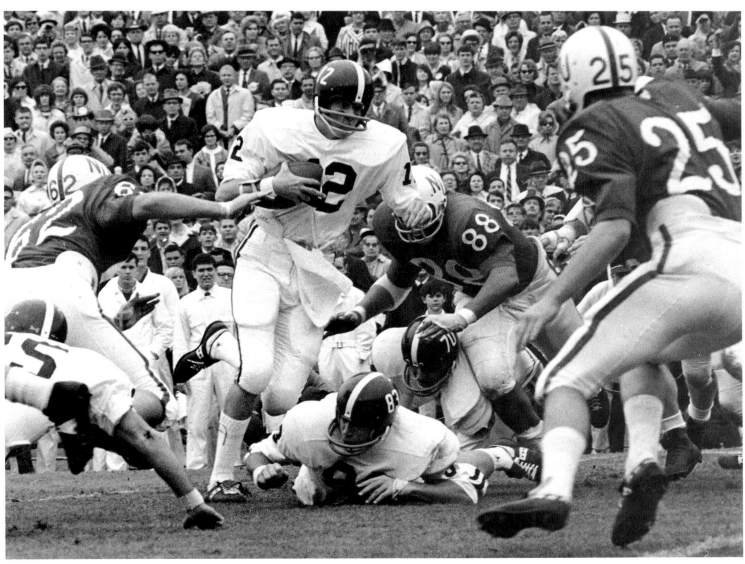

Top: *Alabama's Tyrone King (43) makes an airborne interception of a pass intended for Georgia's Lynn Hunnicut (84) en route to a 25-7 victory in 1972.*

Above: *Bryant gives instructions from his daily perch in "the tower."*

team than his 1965 national champions, but it fell victim to the pollsters who were wrapped up in trying to untangle the Notre Dame-Michigan State situation. Those teams had played to a controversial 10-10 tie in their final game, and Notre Dame was ranked first, the Spartans second. Neither played a post-season game while Alabama again knocked off Nebraska in the Sugar Bowl 34-7, as Perkins, who had caught nine passes for 195 yards in the previous year's victory, caught seven for 178 yards.

Afterward, Bryant called the team "the greatest college football team I've ever seen or been associated with." The poll voters were unmoved and ranked Alabama third, a bitter disappointment to Bryant and his team that was led by Ken Stabler and had turned in some outstanding performances during the year. Stabler hit 16 of 19 passes, nine to Perkins, in a 17-7 victory over Mississippi; and he brought the Tide from a 10-0 deficit against Tennessee with a seven-of-nine burst after not completing a pass earlier in the game. He scored a touchdown, passed for the two-point conversion and set up Steve Davis for the winning field goal in an 11-10 victory.

Bryant's teams took on the Wishbone flavor in the early 1970s, helped by a great running back named Johnny Musso. Nick-

named the "Italian Stallion," Musso held all of Alabama's major all-time rushing records until Bobby Humphrey's seasons in the late 1980s. Playing in 1969-71, Musso gained 2741 yards and scored 34 touchdowns. His final two seasons were his biggest – 1137 yards in 1970 and 1088 in 1971. He accumulated nine 100-yard games in those two years, including 221 against Auburn in 1970. Also a major factor from 1969-71 was David Bailey, the school's top receiver of all time with 132 receptions for 1857 yards and 13 touchdowns.

Musso, along with new quarterback Terry Davis who ran the Wishbone offense, was instrumental in helping Bryant achieve his 200th career victory in a 17-10 triumph over Southern Cal in the opener of the 1971 season. The Tide lost just once in 12 games and won the SEC title, ending the regular season with a 31-7 trouncing of previously unbeaten Auburn as Alabama's defense held the Tigers to just 27 rushing yards. Unbeaten, ranked second, and playing for the national championship when they met top-ranked Nebraska in the Orange Bowl, the Tide's hopes were smashed in a 38-6 loss as three fumbles gave the Huskers a quick 21-0 lead.

But Bryant did win his fourth national championship, according to UPI, two years

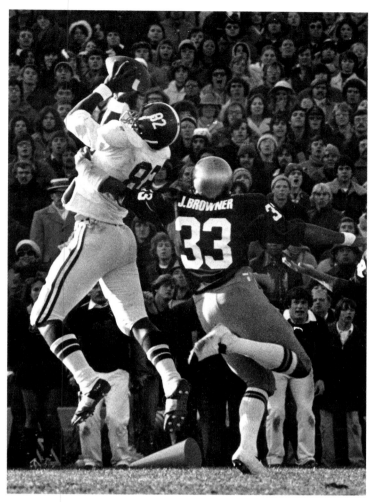

later with another 11-1 season. This team was a scoring machine, with 477 points – the most by any team in Alabama history. Paced by quarterbacks Richard Todd and Gary Rutledge and running back Wilbur Jackson, it rolled up such scores as 66-0 over California, 77-6 over Virginia Tech, 43-13 over Miami, 42-21 against Tennessee, 44-0 against Vanderbilt, and even 35-0 over a fine Auburn team. Its only close call was a 28-14 victory over Georgia when the Tide scored 15 points in the final quarter after trailing 14-13. Alabama then played top-ranked (by AP) Notre Dame in the Sugar Bowl and lost 24-23, a game that is detailed in Chapter 8. Afterward, the Irish were voted Number 1 by AP, but UPI declared the Tide national champs.

In 1978, after Alabama had won six SEC titles in seven seasons, it was AP's turn to crown it national champion after an 11-1 season, the only loss to Southern Cal. This team also had great firepower as quarterback Jeff Rutledge, who often alternated with Steadman Shealy, threw a school-record 30 touchdown passes and had plenty of help from running backs Tony Nathan and Major Ogilvie; the defense featured linebacker E. J. Junior and Marty Lyons. Alabama set the tone for the season when, trailing Nebraska 3-0 in the opening game,

the Tide drove 99 yards for the go-ahead score in a 20-3 victory. Alabama also exacted a bit of revenge for its loss to USC by beating eventual Rose Bowl winner Washington 20-17 two weeks later, and then clinched its national title with a 14-7 victory over Penn State in the Sugar Bowl, a game that is covered in Chapter 8.

Bryant still had one more national championship in him – and it came the following season, when his team was a unanimous selection after its last perfect (12-0) season. Shealy, a clever, gutsy quarterback in the mold of Pat Trammell, guided a great Alabama offense that scored 383 points. It wasn't always easy, though – the Tide had to come from a 17-0 deficit to beat Tennessee 27-17, as Ogilvie scored two touchdowns; Alan McElroy kicked a 27-yard field goal in the third quarter for a 3-0 victory over LSU; and trailing for the only time all season, 18-17 in the fourth quarter of the final game against Auburn, Shealy's eight-yard TD run finally secured a 24-18 win. Still, Alabama was ranked second to Ohio State when it played Arkansas in the Sugar Bowl. The Tide's defense flattened the Razorbacks, stopping them six times on third down and clinching a 24-9 victory and the national title when Ohio State lost in the Rose Bowl.

Above left: *QB Terry Davis (10) ran Alabama's Wishbone offense superbly and led the Tide to a pair of SEC titles in 1971-72.*

Above: *Ozzie Newsome (82) takes to the air to haul in a pass on the Notre Dame 9-yard line late in the fourth quarter of the Notre Dame-Alabama game in 1976.*

Right: *QB Jeff Rutledge led the Tide to its 1978 national championship.*

Far right: *Bear Bryant in a most familiar pre-game pose.*

Below: *Steadman Shealy (with ball) quarterbacked Bryant's final national championship team in 1979.*

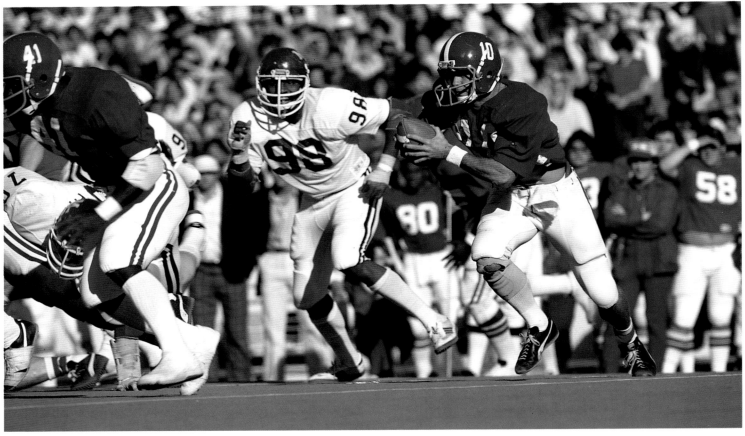

The win at the Sugar Bowl was Bryant's 296th career victory, only 18 off from Amos Alonzo Stagg's all-time record of 314. Bryant was 66 and there was some conjecture as to how long he would continue to coach, but he never hinted that he wanted anything other than to leave with the all-time victory mark. He got Number 300 in a 45-0 romp over Kentucky early in 1980, and the following season achieved his goal.

Glenn (Pop) Warner was the second all-time winner with 313, just one behind Stagg, so on successive weekends in 1981, Bryant hit the high marks. His 313th win, tying Warner, was a 13-10 bumbler over Mississippi State during which the Tide fumbled 11 times but won on freshman Terry Sanders's 28-yard, fourth quarter field goal. Bryant passed Warner and tied Stagg the following week in a 31-16 victory over Penn State as sophomore quarterback Walter Lewis passed for two touchdowns to tight end Jess Bendross. His defense also sacked Penn State QB Todd Blackledge four times and had two goal line stands as the Tide rolled to a 24-3 halftime lead.

Two weeks later in Birmingham, Bryant got his record, in the final game of the season, in a 28-17 victory over arch-rival Auburn. This Alabama team had averaged almost 400 yards per game, but found itself behind 17-14 in the fourth quarter. Lewis erased that on one play, a 38-yard TD pass to Bendross for a 21-17 lead with 10 minutes to play, and the victory was cemented on Lenny Patrick's 15-yard scoring run a few moments later.

Bryant returned for one last season in 1982, and his team sometimes struggled to win eight of 12 games – climaxed by his last game, a victory, in the Liberty Bowl over the University of Illinois.

The Bryant football era ended with that game, and a month later the Bryant era was extinguished when he passed away suddenly, mercifully some said, because he had not known a year of his adult life without football and many wondered what he would have done with no team to coach and no games to win.

Many say that it still isn't the same at Alabama without him.

Top: *Bear Bryant's funeral procession on January 28, 1983 passes by the stadium that now bears his name, where he won 72 games.*

Above: *A huge display of roses marks Bear Bryant's final resting place.*

6. The Tide Rolls On

"Coaching Alabama's football team is the only job I ever really wanted."

That was Ray Perkins's declaration after he was named to succeed Bear Bryant as the Tide's head coach in 1982, and that "yearning" lasted all of five years, until the NFL's Tampa Bay Buccaneers waved a bigger contract at him, when he then declared, "Coaching pro football really is all I've ever wanted to do."

Perkins was coaching the NFL's New York Giants and battling for a division title in 1982 when he suddenly pulled out before the season's end to return to the Capstone. It could well be that Perkins truly longed to return to his alma mater, as succeeding a coach of Bryant's stature, who had been his head coach, was a singular honor.

But circumstances conspired to make his tenure less satisfying than either he, or the Tide's fans, had hoped it would be. Perkins ran into the same wall that has afflicted the successors of other legendary coaches where no matter how successful they may be, it really never is good enough. The Alabama football diehards, numbering in the

Right: *Ray Perkins (shirt and tie), who played on Bear Bryant's 1964-65 national champions, had the impossible task of replacing the most legendary coach in Alabama history. Constantly reminded that he was "no Bear Bryant," Perkins lasted four seasons but guided the Tide to three post-season games.*

Top left: *For over a half-century, Alabama's mascot has been the Red Elephant.*

Above: *Sellout crowds fill both Legion Field in Birmingham and Bryant-Denny Stadium in Tuscaloosa for every game.*

Left: *QB Walter Lewis led Alabama in passing in 1981-83 and ranks second in Tide history with 4257 yards.*

tens of thousands and who filled Bryant-Denny Stadium and Legion Field in Birmingham week after week, often didn't understand that a great coach like Bear Bryant comes along once in a lifetime and that a school simply cannot go out and get "another" Wallace Wade, Frank Thomas, or Bear Bryant. Any illusions that Perkins would achieve that trio's greatness quickly disappeared, and frustrations set in as his teams occasionally fell victim to inconsistencies and lost games that Bryant always seemed to win.

Perkins's teams, from 1983 through 1986, never reached great heights – at least not by the standards used in comparing his achievements to Bryant's – though three of them were invited to, and won, post-season games. A fourth, in 1984, suffered Alabama's first losing season since 1957. Still, Perkins's record was 32-15-1, an average of eight wins per season which at most other schools is cause for rejoicing.

Perkins opened with a 8-4 record, the same as Bryant had in his final season. It included a resounding 28-7 victory over Southern Methodist in the Sun Bowl. His biggest asset was quarterback Walter Lewis, and he added his own imprint with a pro-style passing offense to rev up the Tide's offense. Lewis turned in the best season of his career with 1991 passing yards,

Right: *Quarterback Walter Lewis was Alabama's best all-around offensive performer during the 1980s. He led the team to three post-season games and an SEC title and is Alabama's all-time single season total offense leader with 2329 yards in 1983.*

third best in the school's history; and he finished with 2329 yards of total offense, more than any player ever had produced for Alabama. The team won its first four games, including a solid 20-7 victory over Georgia Tech, ironically coached by Bill Curry, who later succeeded Perkins and who also ran into the "Bryant shadow" problem before he left after the 1989 season.

Against Penn State Lewis threw three touchdown passes, but the Nittany Lions spoiled the honeymoon with a 34-28 victory. Alabama riddled the Nittany Lions' defense for a record 598 yards and roared from a 34-7 deficit in the fourth quarter with 21 straight points, then reached the six-yard line in the final minute before Penn State's defense stopped them. The following week, Tennessee outscored Alabama 10-0 in the

final quarter for a 41-34 victory, and thus began a pattern that eroded Perkins's favor among fans who recalled (or wished to recall) Bryant's teams rarely blowing leads, particularly against fierce rivals.

The weirdest game of the year occurred in Foxboro, Massachusetts against Boston College in an almost surrealistic setting of low, black clouds that had at first poured rain onto the field, and then had given way to thunder and lightning, with temperatures hovering around freezing. All of this was punctuated by a giant lightning bolt that cut off power to the stadium and blanked some of the game from a national television audience on a Friday afternoon of Thanksgiving Day weekend. To add to its discomfort, the Tide also got a taste of "Flutie Magic" as Boston College's quarterback, overcoming a 13-6 Alabama lead, passed for one TD and scored another in the fourth quarter and led the Eagles to a 20-13 victory. The following week, Ricky Moore's 57-yard TD run in the third quarter gave Alabama a 20-16 lead, but Auburn's Bo Jackson answered a short time later with a TD run of 71 yards. Steady rain dampened the offenses of both teams in the fourth quarter, and Auburn had a 23-20 victory. Everything came together in the Sun Bowl, though, when Alabama scored 28 points in the first half as Moore enjoyed his sixth consecutive 100-yard rushing day.

The tone for the 1984 season was set in the opening game when Flutie took his first step en route to the Heisman Trophy and once again burned the Tide. He brought Boston College from a 31-14 deficit early in the third quarter to a 38-31 victory, throw-

ing a touchdown pass and running for another. The Tide lost four of its first five games, and then finished the year with two more losses by a total of three points against LSU and Tennessee. The brightest moment was a 6-0 victory over Penn State. Led by linebackers Cornelius Bennett and Wayne Davis, each of whom had 10 tackles, the Tide allowed the Nittany Lions just 249 yards and broke a scoreless tie in the fourth quarter when Van Tiffin kicked two field goals for all of the Tide's points. The Tide's defense also saved a heroic 17-15 victory over Auburn.

If Alabama broke many hearts during Perkins's tenure, it also stopped a few, as in the first game of the 1985 season against Georgia when quarterback David Shula passed 17 yards to Al Bell for the winning score in the final 15 seconds, and in the final

Left: *David Shula, son of the famed NFL coach, led Alabama's passers in both 1985 and 1986, and threw 29 TD passes during those seasons.*

Above: *Van Tiffin kicked a record 135 consecutive extra points for Alabama, plus 59 field goals, and ranks second in all-time scoring with 312 points. Here he kicks one of those field goals against Ohio State in the 1986 Kickoff Classic during a 16-10 victory.*

game of the year against Auburn when Tiffin's field goal produced a victory with no time to play. The team also salvaged a 14-14 tie against LSU that season when Shula passed two yards to Gene Jelks with 1:24 to play.

The crossroads of the 1985 season came after successive losses to Penn State and Tennessee left the Tide with a 4-2 record. The following week Alabama defeated Memphis State 28-9 as Shula threw for a record four touchdowns, and didn't lose again the rest of the season. A fine 9-2-1 record was capped by a 24-3 victory over Southern Cal in the Aloha Bowl.

Perkins's final season began in the Kickoff Classic at his old stomping grounds in Giants Stadium in New Jersey, against Ohio State, and the Tide owned the fourth quarter this time in a 16-10 victory. This began a seven-game winning streak that included a smashing 28-10 victory over Notre Dame in Birmingham, the first time the Tide had ever beaten the Irish. Shula threw three touchdown passes, and a new star in Alabama's tiara – running back Bobby Humphrey, who became the school's all-time rusher – had 73 yards. The soph runner from Birmingham scored three times and rolled up 217 yards, the most by

any Tide runner since Johnny Musso's 221 yards in 1970, as Alabama scored 42 points in the first half and won a wild 56-28 shootout against Tennessee. Two weeks later he set a school record with 284 yards in 30 carries in a 38-3 victory over Mississippi State.

Penn State's defense smothered Alabama the following week 23-3 at Tuscaloosa, and two weeks later Alabama marched into LSU territory four times in the second half and got only Tiffin's field goal before losing 14-10. Even in the midst of a 7-2 season, the grumbling about Alabama's good-day, bad-day style had begun in earnest and it was clearly audible after the final game of the year when Auburn scored 14 points in the final quarter for a 21-17 victory, the winning points coming in the final 32 seconds.

Perkins was never known for a sense of drama or history, but in the last game he coached at Alabama his 1986 team turned in its best performance in the Sun Bowl, burying Washington 28-6 as Humphrey gained 159 yards and scored a rushing TD while Shula completed 15 of 26 for 176 yards and a pair of touchdowns.

The search for Perkins's successor centered on two factors: whether to find a coach with an Alabama background, or to

nett, Thomas was a tremendous force: five sacks in a 30-10 victory over Texas A&M; eight tackles, three sacks (one for a safety) and eight quarterback "hurries" plus a batted pass in Alabama's 8-3 victory over Penn State; and 14 tackles, four sacks, a blocked punt, and a fumble recovery in a 31-27 victory over Kentucky. That win came in the final 10 seconds on Vince Sutton's three-yard pass to Gene Newberry, capping a last-ditch 86-yard drive and a 24-point fourth quarter. Another nail-biting win was 28-20 over Tennessee when Alabama scored the winning touchdown with 98 seconds to play on Murry Hill's 55-yard run.

Alabama capped the 1988 season with a 29-28 victory over Army in the Sun Bowl, coming from a 28-20 deficit with nine points in the fourth quarter. Quarterback David Smith, who played most of the season on an

Left: *Cornelius Bennett was one of the finest linebackers ever to play at Alabama.*

Below: *Bill Curry served as Alabama coach from 1987-89.*

go outside. The decision to hire Bill Curry, who had never played or coached at Alabama, was never fully accepted by the same diehards who had been so skeptical of Perkins. Like Perkins, neither his success – a notable 26-10-0 record – nor the fact that he was acclaimed for personal integrity were ever fully appreciated.

Curry's first season in 1987 produced a 7-5 record with a 4-1 start that included a 24-13 victory over Penn State, keyed by Humphrey's 220 rushing yards and 73-yard TD. Humphrey scored the winning touchdown on a one-yard run with 46 seconds to play in a 21-18 victory over Mississippi State, the week after he had gained 127 yards and scored twice in a rollicking 41-22 victory over Tennessee. Humphrey had another 177-yard game when Alabama kept the ball for 40 minutes and defeated LSU 22-10, coming from a 10-6 halftime deficit with 16 points in the second half for the win.

Curry's career became a target after a 10-0 loss to Auburn and a 28-24 loss to Michigan in the Hall of Fame game, though the Wolverines only won the game in the final 50 seconds after Humphrey's 17-yard run had helped the Tide to a 24-21 lead with 3:45 to play.

Curry's chances for success in 1988 suffered a severe blow when he lost Humphrey for the final seven games of the season, but a new star had emerged – linebacker Derrick Thomas. Following in the footsteps of another great linebacker, Cornelius Ben-

Above: *Alabama's defense has always been taught to swarm to a ball carrier and John Mangum (29), Steve Webb (84), and Charles Gardner do it against Tennessee during the Tide's victory over the Vols in 1989.*

injured leg that required a cumbersome brace, shattered passing records by completing 33 of 52 passes for 412 yards and four TDs.

The Tide made a gallant run at its first national title since 1979 when it won its first 10 games of the 1989 season. Again, Curry's team was successful against Penn State, winning 17-16 though it took a great play by Thomas to block the Nittany Lions' try for the winning field goal in the final seconds. But even while Alabama was unbeaten and vying for the national championship, Curry's future at Alabama had always been in question; and when the Tide was upset by eleventh-ranked Auburn 30-20, costing them the SEC title outright and a chance for top ranking, and then lost in the Sugar Bowl to the eventual national champion University of Miami, there was not much sentiment for him to remain. He left early in 1990 to become head coach at Kentucky.

Alabama faced the last decade of the century as most of its legion of fans had hoped – with a Bear Bryant disciple in charge of the football program. Gene Stallings, who had played for Bryant at Texas A&M and who later was an assistant coach at Alabama, was named as the school's

22nd football coach – and only the seventh in the last 67 years.

He quickly found that the job posed some problems, as the Tide lost its first three games before rallying to win seven of the last eight and earn a berth in the Fiesta Bowl. But Stallings beat off the critics with two crucial victories in 1990 – 9-6 over Tennessee on Phil Doyle's 48-yard field goal on the game's final play, and 16-7 over Auburn, the first time since 1985 that the Tide had beaten its arch rivals. Against Tennessee, Doyle's third field goal of the day came after Stacy Harrison had blocked a 50-yard field goal by the Vols 95 seconds earlier. Defense was the key to the turnaround, as it was against Auburn – the Tigers' lone TD was just the third that Alabama surrendered in its last seven games. However, the defense didn't hold up in the Fiesta Bowl, as Louisville scored 25 points in the first quarter en route to a 34-7 victory.

Still, as Alabama prepared to celebrate the centennial of its football program in 1992, the future was clearly marked and the Tide's rooters had the man they sought in Gene Stallings – a coach who understands the great Alabama tradition of winning.

Left: *Bobby Humphrey is the most prolific ground-gainer in Alabama's history with 3420 yards in four seasons, including four games of over 200 yards that include an all-time school record 284 against Mississippi State in 1986.*

Left: *Alabama tried to revive the Bear Bryant legend by hiring one of his former pupils and coaches, Gene Stallings, as head coach in 1990. Stallings had played for him at Texas A&M and was an Alabama assistant coach during the 1960s.*

7. Auburn Means War

Every Alabaman will gladly state that a year's happiness depends on who wins the Alabama-Auburn football game. Conference championships, bowl bids, and national championships have been decided year after year when the two teams meet. One writer summed up this series when he wrote: "When the series began in 1893, there was just one ticket booth. Today there are none." That's because the Alabama-Auburn tickets are the most valuable paste-boards in the state, and they are gobbled up early each year so that there is no need for ticket sellers on the day of the game.

The game has featured great perform-ances by outstanding players from both schools: Bobby Marlow, Pat Trammell, Joe Namath, Kenny Stabler, Jeff Rutledge, Tony Nathan, and E. J. Junior for Ala-bama; and Pat Sullivan, Terry Beasley, Tucker Frederickson, Joe Cribbs, and Bo Jackson for Auburn, to say nothing of the great coaching by Frank Thomas and Bear Bryant of Alabama and Ralph (Shug) Jor-dan and Pat Dye of Auburn during most of the past half-century.

But more than anything, the game has been played as a matter of personal pride. It's been that way from the time the schools first played each other in 1893, and espe-

cially since 1948 when the series was re-sumed after a 41-year interruption.

It is almost inconceivable to imagine how this series could have been dropped for more than four decades, particularly after it had gotten off to such a rousing start when the teams decided to play each other after their first season of intercollegiate football, an idea that caught everyone's fancy, even though that first game was played in Birmingham where the Crimson had played its first three games. What did that matter? This was the new era of trans-portation where everyone just jumped on a train, and bingo – you're there.

This series started with a flair from the get-go. The teams played two games in one year and, of course, it didn't take long for the first controversies to arise – two in the first three games. The first game was sche-duled to be played on Washington's Birth-day, 1893, or more than two months after the Tide had played its first three games. To Alabama, this was just the matter of a few open dates before concluding its 1892 sea-son; but to Auburn, it was the first game of the 1893 season, and they disagreed for years until it was finally determined in Alabama's favor.

But on February 22, 1893, the dispute really didn't matter as crowds streamed into Birmingham by train from Montgom-ery, Selma, Anniston, and Eufaula. Auburn, which had split four games in its first season of football, took the game so seriously that it hired F. M. Balliet, who had played at the University of Pennsylva-nia and was then living in Philadelphia, to come and coach its team for this game.

There was an estimated crowd of 2000 cramming Lakeview Park at three o'clock when Alabama's players trotted onto the field for warmups wearing solid white uni-forms, red stockings, and a large red "U of A" on their sweaters. Auburn appeared a moment later, dressed in blue sweaters with an orange "A," white pants, and blue stockings. The game began at 3:30, cer-tainly very late for a football contest in the dead of winter. But the game in those days was totally different from today's sophisti-cated presentation, because the clock rolled right along and there were few stoppages in play. Touchdowns counted four points, extra points two, and the field was 110 yards long.

Auburn won the series' first coin toss and wanted the ball. To this day no one knows who returned the opening kickoff, but J. C. Dunham carried for 10 yards on the first scrimmage play. The star of the game clearly was the Tigers' Rufus Dorsey, who scored three touchdowns, including the first two, on a 20-yard run the second time

Above: *Legion Field in Birmingham, where the Alabama-Auburn game was always played until 1989.*

Left: *Clem Welch (top), Ed Salem (middle), and Gordon Pettus (bottom) score TDs in Alabama's rousing 55-0 victory that renewed the rivalry against Auburn in 1948.*

that Auburn had the ball and a three-yard plunge after Tom Daniels had ripped off a 65-yard run to Alabama's three-yard line. His third was a 65-yard fumble return with the Tide closing in on Auburn's 14-12 lead.

For all the historical significance of this game, finally won by Auburn 32-22, it was also one of the most exciting in the series, because the teams marched up and down the field. The following day, the *Birming-ham News* was moved to note that it was "the greatest football game ever played in the state of Alabama."

It wasn't until midway through the second half, when Daniels scored a pair of touchdowns and kicked both extra points, that Auburn put Alabama away. The Crim-son Tide, coached by Eli Abbott, who also was their best player, stayed right with

Above: *Alabama's Johnny Musso (22) evades Auburn tacklers en route to a 31-7 Tide victory in 1971.*

gomery which offered the schools $600 to make the trip (Alabama got $350 and Auburn $250, even though the Tigers won the game 40-16). Dorsey and Dunham each scored a pair of touchdowns, while Alabama's biggest moment came late in the game when Dave Grayson ran 45 yards for a touchdown.

The second controversy in the history of the rivalry surrounded the game in only the next year, 1894. Both schools accused each other of using players who were not full-time students. Alabama claimed that "Hall of the University of Pennsylvania," and Dorsey, from the previous year's squad, were ineligible. Auburn said that four Alabama players – Abbott, still the team's coach, J. E. Shelley, "and Kirkpatrick and Devin, who had played at North Carolina" – had questionable credentials. Alabama clearly won this skirmish, because both Auburn players did not play while Abbott and Shelley played for the Tide, scoring all of the points in an 18-0 victory.

Alabama had little else to cheer about for the next 13 years, though they upset the Tigers 18-6 in 1903 and scored a decisive 30-0 victory two years later. After the teams played a 6-6 tie in 1907 everyone looked forward to the 1908 game, but it never happened – all because, it is said, of questions of $34 in expense money for the two teams, the geographical selection of an umpire (Auburn wanted a Northerner) and compatible playing dates. As often happens with such minuscule points, charges were hurled back and forth and every time it seemed the matter could be resolved, ill-timed brickbats derailed negotiations.

The consequence was that some of the great teams from both schools never played each other, once moving Alabama's Bear Bryant to note: "We didn't play Auburn when I was a student-athlete at Alabama, so from that standpoint I missed out on some of the tradition of the series. But I can assure you that as a coach, it made me work harder."

The state's legislature gets the credit for resuming the series, because on August 15, 1947 it issued a joint resolution asking the Boards of Trustees for both schools to resume football relations "no later than May 1949." Eight months later the matter was resolved, and the teams scheduled a game on December 8, 1948 in Birmingham's Legion Field, where the series stayed until a home-and-home arrangement was established in 1989.

Alabama welcomed the resumption with a thunderous 55-0 victory as Ed Salem threw three touchdown passes, ran for another score, and kicked six extra points. The following season he teamed with

Auburn. Frank Savage's 10-yard run and William Bankhead's PAT closed an 8-0 Auburn lead to 8-6, and D. H. Smith's 20-yard run only three minutes before half-time followed by Daniels's PAT kept Alabama trailing by just 14-12. "Tuskaloosa" was nonplussed by Dorsey's big fumble return because on Auburn's next possession, team captain W. G. Little sped 35 yards for a TD after Auburn lost a fumble, and G. H. Kyser's PAT again closed the deficit to just two points. Daniels then broke the game open for Auburn.

When the game ended, Delma Wilson, one of Birmingham's "loveliest," presented Daniels, Auburn's captain, with a special cup, admonishing him to "drink from it, and remember the victory that you have won this day." That cup still rests in Auburn's trophy case.

Nine months later, on November 30th, the teams played again, this time in Mont-

sophomore Bobby Marlow for a 34-0 victory. Marlow initially owned Auburn because he scored three touchdowns in both 1950 and 1951, only the third player in the series ever to score three in one game. He also caught a 26-yard TD pass from Salem in the 1950 game while rolling up 113 yards in 24 carries.

The following year, with Auburn's football fortunes at an all-time low (the Tigers won only six of 44 games and were winless in 1950), he was the ultimate difference in Alabama's 25-7 victory. The Tide's defense threw up a goal line stand early in the game, and that set the tone as Marlow's seven-yard TD run shortly afterward gave Alabama a 7-0 lead. He zipped 39 yards for his second score and a 19-0 lead, and capped a day in which he gained 232 rushing yards in 25 carries with a 22-yard scoring run, besting Auburn quarterback Vince Dooley's gutsy performance and spoiling Shug Jordan's debut in this series.

After Jordan became head coach at Auburn in 1951, his teams reeled off five straight victories over the Tide, one of those capping a 1957 national championship. That stopped a year after Bryant's arrival at Alabama, because his great talent for building defensive teams and attracting a "take charge" player helped Alabama dominate the series throughout his tenure. His teams won 19 of 25 games, including nine in a row from 1973 through 1981.

His first victory in 1959, that began a four-game winning streak, was directed by Pat Trammell, who three times led the Tide to victories over Auburn. In 1959 the Tide was a six-point underdog, but Trammell's

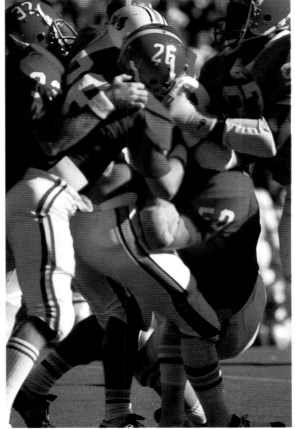

Above: *Bear Bryant's players celebrate his tying Amos Alonzo Stagg's all-time 314-victory mark in 1981 after a victory at Penn State. He established a new mark the following week with a 28-17 victory over arch-rival Auburn.*

Left: *Ironically, after Bear Bryant's teams had beaten Auburn nine times in a row, from 1973-81, the Tigers defeated his last Alabama team 23-22 in 1982, the final game that he coached in this historic rivalry.*

running and passing helped set up a field goal, and then another quarterback, Bobby Shelton, fired a TD pass to Martin Dyess in a 10-0 victory. The next year, helped by Alabama's top-rated defense featuring linebacker Leroy Jordan, a clutch 13-yard pass from Trammell to Bill Battle set up Tommy Brooker's 16-yard field goal in a 3-0 victory. And then in 1961, the Tide capped off its unbeaten national championship season with

Above: *Alabama had scored in 30 consecutive games against Auburn until the Tide lost 10-0 in 1987.*

against Auburn in three appearances, while his understudy for two of these years, Shealy, scored 26 points in three games. Shealy brought Alabama from an 18-17 deficit to a 25-18 victory in 1979 with an eight-yard TD pass. Earlier in the game he had passed for the first touchdown and scored the second on a quarterback sneak.

Of course, Bryant's – and Alabama's – biggest moment in this series occurred in 1981 when he got his 315th career victory, making him the all-time winningest coach at that time. Bear got this one the old-fashioned way: His team earned it, as three different quarterbacks – Alan Gray, Ken Coley, and Lewis – all contributed to the game's first three TDs. Gray ran 63 yards to set up his own touchdown; Coley passed 26 yards to tight end Jesse Bendross for a 14-7 lead; and Lewis hit Bendross with a 38-yard TD pass to overcome a 17-14 Tigers advantage. Linnie Patrick's 15-yard touchdown run secured the 28-17 victory.

The rest of the 1980s weren't always kind to the Tide in its annual battle with Auburn, but the games often were very exciting, as in 1984 and 1985 when, after losing the two previous games against the Tigers by a total of four points, they turned around and won both games by the same difference. In 1984 a 17-15 victory took some of the sting from a losing season, when the Tide's defense rose up and cut down the winning touchdown in the final seconds. Alabama led 17-15 when Auburn intercepted a pass at the 17-yard line, and six plays later faced a fourth-and-goal at the one. But freshman defensive back Rory Turner stopped fullback Brent Fullwood for a three-yard loss to preserve the victory. The following year, Alabama drove for the winning points in the final 57 seconds with Van Tiffin kicking a 52-yard field goal with no time on the clock to get a 25-23 victory.

Alabama thought it had a third straight win in 1986 before wide receiver Lawyer Tillman of Auburn caught a halfback option pass for the winning touchdown with just 32 seconds to play, launching Alabama on a four-game losing streak in this series.

But the rivalry took a historic turn in 1989 when, for the first time ever, the two teams played at Auburn's Jordan-Hare Stadium. The Tigers weren't too hospitable, however, overcoming a 10-7 Alabama lead fashioned on Phil Doyle's 23-yard field goal and an 18-yard touchdown pass from Gary Hollingsworth to Marco Battle, and scored 20 straight points in the second half en route to a 30-20 victory. The loss cost Alabama an unbeaten season and a chance for the Number 1 ranking. But in 1990, the Tide beat the Tigers 16-7 to win back bragging rights for the state of Alabama.

a rousing 34-0 victory, when Trammell and Battle again teamed up to make big plays.

Joe Namath made his debut in the Auburn series in 1962 and tossed two TD passes and scored a third, as Alabama won 38-0. Two years later he capped his career, with the game televised nationally for the first time, by leading Alabama to its second national title of the decade with a 21-14 victory. The Tide trailed 7-6 at halftime, but Ray Ogden's 107-yard run with the second half kickoff and a goal line stand early in the third quarter helped key the comeback win. Namath clinched it with a 23-yard TD pass to future Alabama coach Ray Perkins.

Ken Stabler was the hero in 1967 when he slogged 47 soggy yards on an option sweep play in the third quarter, in only the second time Alabama had the ball in Auburn territory on that rainy, windy afternoon. It was enough for a 7-3 victory, causing Bryant to note quite sagely, "Yes, we were lucky to win the game," and Jordan to note just as sagely, "I don't think the best team won today."

After the Tide blew a 16-3 lead in the final nine-and-a-half minutes of the 1972 game to lose 17-16, Bryant won nine in a row over Auburn as such talented players as Steadman Shealy, Jeff Rutledge, Tony Nathan, and Walter Lewis starred.

In 1978 Rutledge, playing with future NFL stars Nathan and Ozzie Newsome, threw three touchdown passes, the final one establishing a career school record of 30, in a 34-16 victory. He notched six TD passes

Above: *QB Gary Hollingsworth, who had already thrown a TD pass, evades Auburn's pass rush in the 1989 game. Auburn's strong defense denied Alabama its No. 1 ranking and an undisputed SEC title as the Tide fell 30-20.*

Left: *The Tide won back Alabama bragging rights with a 16-7 victory over the Tigers in 1990.*

8. 'Bama And The Bowls

'Bama and the bowls have become one of college football's most enduring marriages. Alabama has played in 43 post-season games in eleven different bowls, from Philadelphia to Pasadena and from Miami to Honolulu, all within the past 55 years. Their record stands at 23 victories, 17 losses, and three ties. The Tide made its first bowl appearance in the 1926 Rose Bowl and, from 1959 through 1983, had a record of 25 straight bowl appearances, the first 24 with Bear Bryant as head coach.

Alabama's bowl history began in the "Granddaddy of them all," the Rose Bowl, in a game that still is ranked as one of the best ever played in that venerable arena. In fact, Alabama's first five appearances came in the Rose Bowl, because it was the only post-season game until the early 1930s. The Tide had swept through the 1925 season unbeaten and untied in nine games under coach Wallace Wade, and then were picked to play the University of Washington, the Pacific Coast Conference's champion, in Pasadena on New Year's Day.

Twenty-two players, urged by university president Dr. Mike Denny to take their books to use in off moments to study for mid-term exams scheduled for early January, left Tuscaloosa for the 2800-mile journey by train. Alabama arrived in California on Christmas Eve to find themselves 10-point underdogs against the Huskies, who were led by All-America back George Wilson. Those odds looked fairly accurate at first, as Wilson propelled Washington to a 12-0 halftime lead.

Injuries forced Wilson from the game for the entire third quarter, during which Alabama roared to eventual victory with a 20-point scoring burst within eight minutes in that period. On Alabama's first play of the second half, Pooley Hubert exploded for 27 yards, and four plays later he had Alabama's first score. Bill Buckler kicked the extra point. On its next offensive play, Grant Gillis passed 59 yards to Johnny Mack Brown, Alabama's All-America running back, for the second touchdown. "All I had to do was sidestep one man and I was across," Brown said later. Lightning struck again on the next series when Hubert told Brown to run as fast as he could toward the end zone. "When I reached the three, I

Below: *Alabama's rich bowl history began with five appearances in the Rose Bowl. Here, the unbeaten 1937 team limbers up a few days before playing California where it suffered its first post-season loss, 13-0.*

looked around and the ball was coming down over my shoulder," Brown said. "I took it in stride, stiff-armed one tackler and carried another over the goal line with me." That was it, as Alabama went on to win 20-19.

The Tide returned to Pasadena the following season to play a 7-7 tie against Stanford. Three years later, the Tide bade farewell to Wade in the Rose Bowl with a resounding 24-0 victory over Washington State's "Wonder Team" to climax a third unbeaten season. A 61-yard reverse pass from end Jimmy Moore to John Suther got the first touchdown in the second quarter, after Wade had stunned everyone by starting his second team, or "shock troops." Moore used the same play again for 46 yards to set up Monk Campbell's one-yard TD. Campbell then polished off a 21-point second quarter with a 43-yard touchdown run.

Dixie Howell, Don Hutson, and Bear Bryant popped a few eyeballs in the 1935 Rose Bowl as Alabama beat Stanford 29-13. Stanford's Bobby Grayson gave the Indians a quick lead in the first quarter before Howell took over the offensive show in a fitting climax to his great career. He scored on a six-yard run. Riley Smith missed the PAT, but a few moments later kicked a field goal as part of a 22-point second quarter, that was triggered by 256 yards of offense. Howell got 96 passing with four completions to Hutson and three to Bryant, and added 96 rushing, including a 67-yard TD for a 16-7 lead.

Throughout their time preparing for Stanford, Thomas and the Tide were constantly peppered with the spectre of Minnesota, which also had been considered for the Rose Bowl. Before the game began, thousands of Stanford fans began chanting, "We want Minnesota." But when Howell's 67-yard touchdown run gave Alabama a 16-7 lead in the third quarter, the Tide's rooters got their revenge with a mighty putdown by roaring, "We want Minnesota."

At the same time, either Stanford over-

Top: *Alabama came from behind to beat Boston College 37-21 in the 1943 Orange Bowl. BC's Mike Holovak muffs a pass as a Tide defender closes in.*

Above: *Norwood Hodges scores vs. Duke in the 1945 Sugar Bowl.*

Right: *In their final trip to the Rose Bowl, in 1946, the Tide defeated Southern Cal 34-14. Harry Gilmer, at the bottom of this pile after a one-yard TD plunge, also passed for a touchdown, one of three that he threw in post-season games.*

valued its own defense or it didn't believe Alabama was a good offensive team, because it chose to kick off after the first two Alabama scores, and each time the Tide rolled in for more points.

The most electrifying points came eight seconds before the end of the first half when coach Frank Thomas sent on quarterback Tilden Campbell, who was more conservative than Smith, with the expectation that he would call a simple running play to wind down the clock. But Campbell had decided on the sideline that he wanted to pass, and went out and worked a 54-yard touchdown pass to Joe Riley for a 22-7 lead.

With the Tide ahead 22-13 in the second half, Thomas's second decision to be conservative also met with different results. He sent Hutson into the game to tell Smith not to throw any more passes. "The trouble was," Hutson recalled, "since it was the first play I was in, I couldn't talk – especially with the referee right there in the huddle. So Riley figured I'd been sent in to catch a pass and he called one."

This became the game's final score, a 39-yard play as Hutson took advantage of Stanford defensive back Bones Hamilton who three times earlier in the game saw him catch the ball in front of him. This time, he raced up to make an interception only to see Hutson zip past him on the out-side to catch the touchdown pass.

Alabama made two more Rose Bowl appearances before the Classic entered into its still-existing pact with the Big Ten (one can only imagine how many trips Alabama would have made had the Rose Bowl stayed "open"). Stymied by a total of eight turnovers, the Tide lost to California 13-0 in 1938. Alabama didn't return to Pasadena until 1946, then exploded with Harry Gilmer to bury Southern California 34-14. The Tide's defense held USC to minus 24 yards in the first half and just 41 overall while rolling up 351 yards as Gilmer passed for a touchdown and added 116 yards rushing.

Alabama has appeared in 11 Sugar Bowls, the most by any college team, thanks in part to the bowl's hookup with the Southeastern Conference champion. There have been good and bad times, but perhaps none so agonizingly memorable as the first Sugar Bowl appearance in 1945 when the Tide's "War Babies" lost to Duke 29-26. Harry Gilmer's passing set up three touchdowns in the first half and a 19-13 lead, and Hugh Morrow's 75-yard interception return gave the Tide a 26-20 lead in the fourth quarter.

Thomas decided to play it safe when Alabama was pinned into its own territory late in the game and took a deliberate safety, figuring that his team could get off a long

Left: *Alabama's Bob Conway returns a kickoff following Syracuse's only touchdown in the Tide's 61-6 romp in the 1953 Orange Bowl.*

Below: *Tim Davis kicks the first of four field goals in Alabama's 12-7 win over Ole Miss in the 1964 Sugar Bowl.*

free kick. He also assumed the coverage would be good enough to keep Duke away from the end zone. John Wade's punt carried 40 yards, but the coverage broke down and Duke returned the ball 20 yards to set up the winning touchdown.

Alabama won its first Sugar Bowl with a 10-3 victory over Arkansas in 1962 on Pat Trammell's 12-yard touchdown run that was set up by Mike Fracchia's 43-yard run. Tim Davis later added a 32-yard field goal. On an even happier note, in 1978, with the national championship at stake, Alabama defeated top-ranked Penn State 14-7 as Jeff Rutledge passed 30 yards to Bruce Bolton for a first-half TD. Alabama broke a 7-7 tie in the third quarter when Lou Ikner returned a punt 62 yards to Penn State's 11-yard line, and Major Ogilvie sped eight yards for the TD. But the defense finally won the game, turning back Penn State twice inside the one-yard line late in the fourth quarter, the last time when linebacker Barry Krauss stuffed Mike Guman on fourth down at the goal line. "That goal line stand was something I'll never forget," Bryant said later.

There were other happy times, as well. Three years earlier, in 1975, Alabama had gone to the Sugar Bowl and finally exorcised whatever post-season devils that had caused eight straight winless post-season

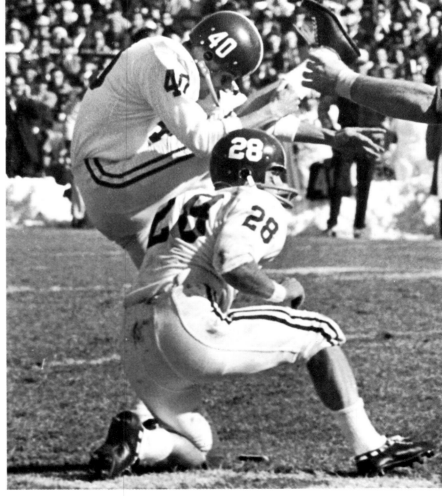

appearances by beating Penn State 13-6 with a 10-point fourth quarter. Richard Todd had a spectacular game with 10 of 12 passes for 205 yards, including one of 55 yards to Ozzie Newsome that set up Mike Stock's 11-yard touchdown run. And in 1979 Alabama won 12 games in a season for the first time ever by beating Arkansas 24-9 in the Sugar Bowl, thus nailing down a national championship.

Post-season bowl games carried added importance from the late 1960s onward, as the various polls used those results to determine which team would be national champion. In addition to its victory over Penn State in 1979, Alabama won the 1965 national title after beating Nebraska 39-28 in the Orange Bowl, thanks to a pair of TD passes from Steve Sloan to Ray Perkins. Les Kelley's four-yard TD run broke a 7-7 tie in the second quarter and the Tide was off and running. In a rematch the following year without a title on the line, Alabama won 34-7 in the Sugar Bowl.

The Sugar Bowl also was the site of one of the most painfully memorable of all Alabama post-season games when the Tide lost a national championship in a razor-thin 24-23 loss to Notre Dame in 1973. Alabama was Number 1 going into the game, the Irish ranked third and fourth in the two wire service polls. Everything boiled down to the final minutes when Notre Dame led 24-23, and an Alabama punt put the ball at the Irish two-yard line. Bryant felt his defense could keep the Irish bottled up and get him good field position for one last scoring drive. But on third down, Notre Dame quarterback Tom Clements fooled Alabama's defense and passed 35 yards to tight end Robin Weber, foiling any Alabama comeback try. Notre Dame won the game and was selected national champion.

The teams replayed the drama the following year in the Orange Bowl, and again Notre Dame won 13-11, in coach Ara Parseghian's final game. Notre Dame scored all of its points in the first half. Todd brought the Tide to 13-11 with a 48-yard TD pass to Russ Schamun and a two-point conversion to George Pugh, but saw a last-ditch scoring drive spoiled by a Notre Dame interception, one of four turnovers suffered by the Tide that evening.

There were other memorable moments as well in Alabama's bowl history, but none as famous as Tommy Lewis's jumping off the Alabama bench to tackle Rice's Dickie Moegle in the 1954 Cotton Bowl. Lewis had given the Tide a 6-0 lead in the first quarter and had just returned to the bench after Alabama was foiled deep in Rice territory. Deeply engrossed in reflecting on his team's failure as he sat on the bench, he looked up

in time to see Moegle, who had scored earlier on a 79-yard run, sweep right end and head into the open. In a reflex action, he jumped up, ran onto the field and tumbled Moegle with a shoulder tackle and then quickly returned to the bench, stunned by his own action. Referee Cliff Shaw then picked up the ball and set it up for the extra point, awarding Moegle a 95-yard TD run.

At the halftime break Lewis went to Rice's dressing room to apologize, and Rice coach Jess Neely consoled him. "My heart went out to him," Neely said later. "I told him, 'Don't let it bother you.'"

"I'm too emotional," Lewis said after the game. "I kept telling myself, 'I didn't do it, I didn't do it.' But I knew I had. I'm just too full of Alabama. He just ran too close. I know I'll hear about it for the rest of my life."

Alabama's first Cotton Bowl appearance – its first post-season game outside the Rose Bowl – was memorable for other reasons. In a 1942 encounter against Texas A&M, the Tide turned a dozen turnovers into 29 points in a 29-21 victory. Alabama had only one first down for the entire game, was buried offensively 309-75, completed just one pass compared to 13 by the Aggies, and ran only 32 plays to A&M's 79. Still, Frank Thomas's team led 29-7 into the fourth quarter as Jimmy Nelson returned a punt 72 yards for a TD and a fumble 21 yards for another; Holt Rast got a 10-yard intercep-

tion TD; and Don Whitmire's fumble recovery set up Russ Craft's eight-yard TD.

Joe Namath also had a pair of memorable games in his two post-season appearances (as noted in Chapter 5, he was suspended by Bryant for disciplinary reasons in the Tide's 1964 Sugar Bowl appearance). In the 1963 Orange Bowl Namath, then a sophomore, led Alabama to a 17-0 victory over Oklahoma. He ended a 10-play, 61-yard first-quarter touchdown drive with a five-yard scoring pass to Dick Williamson; set up the other touchdown with a 20-yard pass

Opposite: *In one of the strangest moments in bowl history, Tommy Lewis (42, dark jersey) leaves the sideline (top photo) as Rice's Dick Moegle passes Alabama's bench on his way to an apparent TD in the 1954 Cotton Bowl. (Middle and bottom photos) Lewis tackles him near the 40-yard line, but Moegle was awarded the score and Rice went on to win 28-6.*

Above: *Joe Namath, playing on a gimpy leg, completed 18 of 37 for 255 yards and two TDs in the 1965 Orange Bowl against Texas.*

Left: *Major Ogilvie skips through the Baylor defense during Alabama's 30-2 victory in the 1981 Cotton Bowl.*

Above: *Gene Stallings, flanked by two of his players, led the Tide to a berth in the Fiesta Bowl in his first season as head coach.*

Opposite: *No one enjoys Alabama's bowl games more than its fans, shown parading down New Orleans' Bourbon Street before the 1990 Sugar Bowl.*

to Williamson before Cotton Clark sped 15 yards around right end for the score; and set up Tim Davis's 19-yard field goal.

Like the Sugar Bowl, games in the Orange Bowl also have some special appeal for Alabama. The first time they played there, in 1943, the Tide roared back from a 12-0 first-quarter deficit to bury Boston College 37-21. The Tide, as so often was its habit, had a second-quarter explosion, this time for 22 points, with George Hecht's 21-yard field goal providing a 22-21 halftime lead following Russ Mosley's 14-yard TD pass to Wheeler Leeth; one of 17 yards from Johnny August to Ted Cook; and Bobby Jenkins's 40-yard run that set up his one-yard TD run.

In the 1965 Orange Bowl, only a few weeks before signing a record $427,000 contract with the New York Jets of the National Football League and playing with a knee injury so painful he was unable to start the game, Namath lost a shootout against Texas that also cost Alabama a

national title. He had a spectacular day despite the 21-17 loss, completing 18 of 37 passes for 255 yards and two touchdowns, 74 yards to Wayne Trimble and 20 to Ray Perkins, while being chosen as the game's Most Valuable Player. He almost won the game before Texas linebacker Tommy Nobis stopped him on the goal line as he tried a quarterback sneak for the winning points.

Of course, the Liberty Bowl also has played a role in Alabama's bowl history. Bear Bryant coached his first post-season game for Alabama in the 1959 inaugural game in Philadelphia, and lost to Penn State 7-0. In 1982 he also coached his last game for Alabama in the Liberty Bowl, defeating Illinois 21-15 in Memphis, for his 323rd victory. Jeremiah Castile's three interceptions were the big plays for the Tide, the final one snuffing out a last-ditch Illini drive.

And the beat still goes on in post-season. College football just wouldn't be the same without 'Bama and the bowls.

Alabama Crimson Tide Football Records

YEAR-BY-YEAR RESULTS

Year	Coach	W	L	T	Pts	Opp	Year	Coach	W	L	T	Pts	Opp
1892	E. N. Beaumont	2	2	0	96	37	1941	Frank W. Thomas	9	2	0	263	85
1893	Eli Abbott	0	4	0	24	74	1942	Frank W. Thomas	8	3	0	246	97
1894	Eli Abbott	3	1	0	60	16	1943	No Team					
1895	Eli Abbott	0	4	0	12	112	1944	Frank W. Thomas	5	2	2	272	83
1896	Otto Wagonhurst	2	1	0	56	10	1945	Frank W. Thomas	10	0	0	430	80
1897	Allen McCants	1	0	0	6	0	1946	Frank W. Thomas	7	4	0	186	110
1898	No Team						1947	H. D. Drew	8	3	0	210	101
1899	W. A Hartin	3	1	0	39	31	1948	H. D. Drew	6	4	1	228	170
1900	M. Griffin	2	3	0	52	99	1949	H. D. Drew	6	3	1	227	130
1901	M. H. Harvey	2	1	2	92	23	1950	H. D. Drew	9	2	0	328	107
1902	Eli Abbott,						1951	H. D. Drew	5	6	0	263	188
	J. O. Heyworth	4	4	0	191	49	1952	H. D. Drew	10	2	0	325	139
1903	W. B. Blount	3	4	0	60	114	1953	H. D. Drew	6	3	3	178	152
1904	W. B. Blount	7	3	0	100	62	1954	H. D. Drew	4	5	2	123	104
1905	Jack Leavenworth	6	4	0	178	113	1955	J. B. Whitworth	0	10	0	48	256
1906	J. W. H. Pollard	5	1	0	97	82	1956	J. B. Whitworth	2	7	1	85	208
1907	J. W. H. Pollard	5	1	2	70	64	1957	J. B. Whitworth	2	7	1	69	173
1908	J. W. H. Pollard	6	1	1	108	31	1958	Paul W. Bryant	5	4	1	106	75
1909	J. W. H. Pollard	5	1	2	68	17	1959	Paul W. Bryant	7	2	2	95	59
1910	Guy S. Lowman	4	4	0	65	107	1960	Paul W. Bryant	8	1	2	183	56
1911	D. V. Graves	5	2	2	153	31	1961	Paul W. Bryant	11	0	0	297	25
1912	D. V. Graves	5	3	1	156	55	1962	Paul W. Bryant	10	1	0	289	39
1913	D. V. Graves	6	3	0	188	40	1963	Paul W. Bryant	9	2	0	227	95
1914	D. V. Graves	5	4	0	211	64	1964	Paul W. Bryant	10	1	0	250	88
1915	Thomas Kelly	6	2	0	250	51	1965	Paul W. Bryant	9	1	1	256	107
1916	Thomas Kelly	6	3	0	156	62	1966	Paul W. Bryant	11	0	0	301	44
1917	Thomas Kelly	5	2	1	168	29	1967	Paul W. Bryant	8	2	1	204	131
1918	No Team						1968	Paul W. Bryant	8	3	0	184	139
1919	Xen C. Scott	8	1	0	280	22	1969	Paul W. Bryant	6	5	0	314	268
1920	Xen C. Scott	10	1	0	377	35	1970	Paul W. Bryant	6	5	1	334	264
1921	Xen C. Scott	5	4	2	241	104	1971	Paul W. Bryant	11	1	0	368	122
1922	Xen C. Scott	6	3	1	300	81	1972	Paul W. Bryant	10	2	0	406	150
1923	Wallace Wade	7	2	1	222	50	1973	Paul W. Bryant	11	1	0	477	113
1924	Wallace Wade	8	1	0	290	24	1974	Paul W. Bryant	11	1	0	329	96
1925	Wallace Wade	10	0	0	297	26	1975	Paul W. Bryant	11	1	0	374	72
1926	Wallace Wade	9	0	1	249	27	1976	Paul W. Bryant	9	3	0	327	140
1927	Wallace Wade	5	4	1	154	73	1977	Paul W. Bryant	11	1	0	380	139
1928	Wallace Wade	6	3	0	187	75	1978	Paul W. Bryant	11	1	0	345	168
1929	Wallace Wade	6	3	0	196	58	1979	Paul W. Bryant	12	0	0	383	67
1930	Wallace Wade	10	0	0	271	13	1980	Paul W. Bryant	10	2	0	352	98
1931	Frank W. Thomas	9	1	0	370	57	1981	Paul W. Bryant	9	2	1	296	151
1932	Frank W. Thomas	8	2	0	200	51	1982	Paul W. Bryant	8	4	0	317	201
1933	Frank W. Thomas	7	1	1	130	17	1983	Ray Perkins	8	4	0	366	229
1934	Frank W. Thomas	10	0	0	316	45	1984	Ray Perkins	5	6	0	226	208
1935	Frank W. Thomas	6	2	1	185	55	1985	Ray Perkins	9	2	1	318	181
1936	Frank W. Thomas	8	0	1	168	35	1986	Ray Perkins	10	3	0	351	163
1937	Frank W. Thomas	9	1	0	225	33	1987	Bill Curry	7	5	0	268	213
1938	Frank W. Thomas	7	1	1	149	40	1988	Bill Curry	9	3	0	317	188
1939	Frank W. Thomas	5	3	1	101	53	1989	Bill Curry	10	2	0	332	184
1940	Frank W. Thomas	7	2	0	166	80	1990	Gene Stallings	7	5	0	260	162

TOP CAREER RUSHERS

	Att	Yds	Avg
1. Bobby Humphrey (1985-88)	615	3420	5.6
2. Johnny Musso (1969-71)	574	2741	4.8
3. Bobby Marlow (1950-52)	408	2560	6.3
4. Johnny Davis (1974-77)	447	2519	5.6
5. Ricky Moore (1981-84)	469	2270	4.8

TOP CAREER RECEIVERS

	Rec	Yds	Avg	TD
1. David Bailey (1969-71)	132	1857	14.1	13
2. Ozzie Newsome (1974-77)	102	2070	20.3	16
3. Dennis Homan (1965-67)	87	1495	17.2	18
4. Jesse Bendross (1980-83)	76	1359	17.9	11
5. Joey Jones (1980-83)	71	1386	19.5	13

TOP CAREER PASSERS

	Att-Com	Yds	TD	Int
1. Scott Hunter (1968-70)	672-382	4899	27	32
2. Walter Lewis (1980-83)	504-286	4257	29	27
3. David Shula (1984-86)	578-313	4069	35	30
4. Jeff Rutledge (1975-78)	372-207	3351	30	23
5. Harry Gilmer (1944-47)	407-215	2863	26	22

TOP CAREER SCORERS

	TD	PAT	FG	Pts
1. Phillip Doyle (1987-90)	—	105	78	339
2. Van Tiffin (1983-86)	—	135	59	312
3. R. Humphrey (1985-88)	40	2	—	240
4. Johnny Musso (1969-71)	34	4	—	212
5. Bill Davis (1971-73)	—	133	26	211

BOWL RESULTS

The Aloha Bowl – Honolulu, Hawaii
Record: Won 1, Lost 0
1985 – Alabama 24, Southern Cal 3

The Astro-Bluebonnet Bowl – Houston, Texas
Record: Won 0, Lost 0, Tied 2
1960 – Alabama 3, Texas 3
1970 – Alabama 24, Oklahoma 24

The Cotton Bowl – Dallas, Texas
Record: Won 2, Lost 4
1942 – Alabama 29, Texas A&M 21
1954 – Rice 28, Alabama 6
1968 – Texas A&M 20, Alabama 16
1973 – Texas 17, Alabama 13
1981 – Alabama 30, Baylor 2
1982 – Texas 14, Alabama 12

The Fiesta Bowl – Tempe, Arizona
Record: Won 0, Lost 1
1991 – Louisville 35, Alabama 7

The Gator Bowl – Jacksonville, Florida
Record: Won 0, Lost 1
1968 – Missouri 35, Alabama 10

The Hall of Fame Bowl – Tampa, Florida
Record: Won 0, Lost 1
1988 – Michigan 28, Alabama 24

The Liberty Bowl – Philadelphia & Memphis
Record: Won 2, Lost 2
1959 – Penn State 7, Alabama 0
1969 – Colorado 47, Alabama 33
1976 – Alabama 36, UCLA 6
1982 – Alabama 21, Illinois 15

The Orange Bowl – Miami, Florida
Record: Won 4, Lost 3
1943 – Alabama 37, Boston College 21
1953 – Alabama 61, Syracuse 6
1963 – Alabama 17, Oklahoma 0
1965 – Texas 21, Alabama 17
1966 – Alabama 39, Nebraska 28
1972 – Nebraska 38, Alabama 6
1975 – Notre Dame 13, Alabama 11

The Rose Bowl – Pasadena, California
Record: Won 4, Lost 1, Tied 1
1926 – Alabama 20, Washington 19
1927 – Alabama 7, Stanford 7
1931 – Alabama 24, Washington State 0
1935 – Alabama 29, Stanford 13
1938 – California 13, Alabama 0
1946 – Alabama 34, Southern Cal 14

The Sugar Bowl – New Orleans, Louisiana
Record: Won 7, Lost 4
1945 – Duke 29, Alabama 26
1948 – Texas 27, Alabama 7
1962 – Alabama 10, Arkansas 3
1964 – Alabama 12, Mississippi 7
1967 – Alabama 34, Nebraska 7
1973 – Notre Dame 24, Alabama 23
1975 – Alabama 13, Penn State 6
1978 – Alabama 35, Ohio State 6
1979 – Alabama 14, Penn State 7
1980 – Alabama 24, Arkansas 9
1990 – Miami (FL) 33, Alabama 25

The Sun Bowl – El Paso, Texas
Record: Won 3, Lost 0
1983 – Alabama 28, SMU 7
1986 – Alabama 28, Washington 6
1988 – Alabama 29, Army 28

Composite Bowl Record:
Won 23, Lost 17, Tied 3

Index

Page numbers in italics refer to illustrations

Abbott, Eli, 10, *12*, 12, 13, 65, 66
Aloha Bowl, 60
Angelich, Jim, *31*, 31, 32
Arkansas, University of, 43, 45, 49, 53, 73
Army *14*, 61
Auburn University, 7, 13, 14, *36*, 37, 39, 45, 48, 52, 53, 55, 59, 60, 61, *64*, 64-68
August, Johnny, 76
Avery, Bart, 34

Bailey, David, 52
Balliet, F. M., 65
Bankhead, William, *10*, 10, 66
Barnes, Emile "Lovely", *21*, 24
Battle, Bill, 67, 68
Battle, Marco, 68
Bay, Bill, 17
Baylor University, 75
Beasley, Terry, 64
Beaumont, Eugene, 10, 12, *13*
Bell, Al, 59
Bendross, Jesse, 55, 68
Bennett, Cornelius, 8, 59, 61, *61*
Bernier, Charles, *15*, 15
Blackledge, Todd, 55
Blackman, Sumpter, 34
Bolton, Bruce, 73
Boston College, 34, 58, 59, 71, 76
Boswell, Charley, 34
Bowdoin, James "Goofy", 24
Brooker, Tommy, 67
Brown, Dave, 34
Brown, Johnny Mack, 7, 18, *19*, *21*, 21, 24, 37, 70, 71
Brown, Red, *22-23*, 24
Bryant, Paul "Bear", 6, 8, *9*, 19, 28, 31, *31*, 35, 41, *42*, *43*, 42-55, *46-47*, *48*, *49*, *52*, *54*, *55*, 56, 57, 58, 62, 64, 66, *67*, 67, 68, 70, 71, 73, 74, 75, 76
Bryant-Denny Stadium, 7, 17, *57*, 57
Buckler, Bill, 18, 21, 70
Butts, Wally, 48

Cain, John "Sugar", 25, *28*, 29, 31
Caldwell, Herschel "Rosey", 18, 21, 24
California-Berkeley, University of, 32, 53, 72
California, University of Southern, 32, 35, 36, 48, 53, 72
Cammack, Gillis, 37
Camp, Walter, 10
Campbell, "Monk", *25*, 25, 71, 72
Cannon, Billy, 38, 44
Casteal, David, 39
Castile, Jeremiah, 76
Clark, Cotton, 76
Clemens, Al, 17
Clements, Tom, 74
Clemson University, 24, 32
Coley, Ken, 68
Colgate University, 21
Conway, Bob, *73*
Cook, Ted, 76
Cope, Robert E. L., 12
Cotton Bowl, 8, 34, 41, 74, 75
Craft, Russ, 34, 75
Cribbs, Joe, 64
Crisp, Hank, 15

Cummings, Joe, 41
Curry, Bill, 58, *61*, 62

Daniels, Tom, 65, 66
Davies, Marion, *21*
Davis, Steve, 52
Davis, Terry, 52, *53*
Davis, Tim, 48, *73*, 73, 76
Davis, Wayne, 59
Demyanovich, Joe, *31*, 31, 34
Denny, Dr. George "Mike", 6, 16, *17*, 17, 26, 27, 70
Dietzel, Paul, 44
Dodd, Bobby, 45
Dooley, Vince, 67
Dorsey, Rufus, 65, 66
Doyle, Phil, 62, 68
Drew, Harold "Red", 6, 28, 31, 36-41, *37*, *38*
Dudley, Bud, 44
Duke University, 24, 26, 35, *71*, 72, 73
Dunham, J. C., 65, 66
Dye, Pat, 64
Dyess, Martin, 44, 67

Eberdt, Jess, 24
Enis, Ben, 24

Feathers, Beattie, 29, 31
Ferguson, Burr, 12
Fiesta Bowl, 62, 76
Florida, University of, 19, 39
Flutie, Doug, 58, 59
Fordham University, 34
Fracchia, Mike, 45, *45*, 73
Francis, Kavanaugh, *31*
Frazier, Tom, 12
Frederickson, Tucker, 64
Fullwood, Brent, 68

Gammon, George, 34
Gardner, Charles, *62*
Georgia, University of, 14, 16, 21, 25, 26, 32, 35, 41, 45, 49, *52*, 59
Georgia Tech, 19, 21, 24, 39, 45, 58
Gillis, Grant, 21, 70
Gilmer, Harry, 7, 27, 34, 35, *35*, 36, 37, 45, *72*, 72
Graves, D. V. "Bibb", 10, *15*, 15
Gray, Alan, 68
Grayson, Bobby, 32, 71
Grayson, D. A., 12, 13, 66
Guman, Mike, 73

Hall, Galen, 44
Hamilton, Bones, 72
Harrell, Billy, 34
Harrison, Stacy, 62
Harvey, M. H., 14
Hecht, George, 76
Helms Athletic Foundation, 21, 24
Hill, Buster, 41
Hill, Murry, 61
Hobson, Clell, *39*, 39, 41
Hollingsworth, Gary 68, *69*
Holovak, Mike, *71*
Homan, Dennis, 48, 49
Hoover, Pres. Herbert, *26*
Howard, Frank, 24
Howell, Millard "Dixie", 7, *27*, *28*, *30*, *31*, 31, 32, 34, 35, 37, 43, 71
Hubert, Pooley, 17, 18, 21, 24, 70
Hughes, Howard, 34
Humphrey, Bobby, *1*, 4, 7, 38, 52, 60, 61, *63*
Hunnicut, Lynn, *52*
Hunter, Scott, 43
Hurlbut, Jack, 48
Hutson, Don, 7, 27, *31*, 31, *32*, 32, *42*, 43, 71, 72

Ikner, Lou, 73
Illinois, University of, 55, 76
Ingram, Hootie, *41*, 41

Jackson, Bo, 59, 64
Jackson, Bobby, 44
Jackson, Wilbur, 53
Jelks, Gene, 60
Jenkins, Bobby, *34*, 34, 76
Johns, Willie, 37
Jones, Bruce, 21
Jordan, Leroy, 45, 67, 68
Jordan, Ralph "Shug", 64, 67
Junior, E. J., 53, 64

Kentucky, University of, 19, 32, 43, 61, 62
Kilgrow, Joe, 32, *33*
King, Tyrone, *52*
Kochman, Roger, 44
Krauss, Barry, 73
Kyser, G. H. "Hub", 12, 66

Layne, Bobby, 36
Lee, Bill, 28, *29*, *31*, 31
Leeth, Wheeler, 76
Legion Field, Birmingham, AL, 7, 57, *57*, *65*
Lewis, Tommy, 8, *38*, *39*, 39, *40*, 74, *75*, 75
Lewis, Walter, 8, 55, 57, *57*, *58*, 58, 68
Liberty Bowl, 55, 76
Little, W. G., 10, *11*, 12, 66
Louisiana State University, 21, 24, 38, 41, 44, 53, 59, 60, 61
Louisville, University of, 62
Luna, Bobby, *39*, 39
Lyons, Marty, 53

McClendon, Charlie, 44
McElroy, Alan, 53
McGugin, Dan, 19, 24
Mancha, Vaughan, 35
Mangum, John, *62*
Marcus, Van, 41
Marlow, Bobby, 37, *39*, 64, 67
Marr, Charlie, *31*
Martin, Gary, 48
Maryland, University of, 40, 43
Memphis State University, 60
Miami, University of, 48, 53, 62
Michigan, University of, 61
Michigan State University, 49, 52
Miller, John, 24
Mims, Carl, 34
Minnesota, University of, 71
Mississippi, University of, 13, 21, 40, 46, 48, *50-51*, 52, 73
Mississippi State University, 17, 21, 24, 31, 35, 41, 49, 55, 60, 63
Moegle, Dickie, 8, 41, 74, 75, *75*
Monsky, Leroy, 32
Moore, Jimmy, 25, 71
Moore, Ricky, 59
Morrow, Bill, *31*
Morrow, Hugh, *72*
Moseley, Herkey, 32
Moseley, Ross, 34
Mosley, Russ, 76
Musso, Johnny, 7, 38, 39, 52, 60, *67*

Namath, Joe, 7, 43, 45, *45*, 48, 48, 64, 68, *75*, 75, 76
Nathan, Tony, 53, 64, 68
Navy, 17
Nebraska, University of, 49, 52, 53, 74
Neely, Jess, 75
Neighbors, Billy, 45
Nelson, Jimmy, 34, 75
Newberry, Gene, 61
Newsome, Ozzie, *53*, 68, 74
Neyland, Gen. Bob, 29

Nobis, Tommy, 76
Notre Dame University, 25, 26, 27, 28, 35, 36, 48, 52, 53, 60, 74

O'Dell, Richard, 45
Ogden, Ray, 48, 68
Ogilvie, Major, 53, 73, *75*
Ohio State University, 36, 53, 60
Oklahoma, University of, 43, 75
Oklahoma State University, 41
Orange Bowl, 34, 39, 41, 48, 49, 52, 71, 73, 74, 75, 76

Pacific Coast Conference, 21, 70
Papas, Julius, 34
Parseghian, Ara 74
Patrick, Lenny, 55, 68
Paty, Dr. Raymond, 35
Pennsylvania, University of, 10, 13, 16, 17, 18, 65, 66
Pennsylvania State University, 17, 44, 53, 55, 58, 59, 60, 61, 62, 67, 73, 74, 76
Perkins, Ray, *9*, *56*, 56-61, 68, 74, 76
Pollard, J. W. H. "Doc", *14*, 14
Pratt, Derrill, *14*, 15
Pratt, H. M., 12
Probst, Short, 17
Pugh, George, 74

Rast, Holt, 75
Ray, David, 49
"Red Elephant", *6*, *57*
Rice, Bill, *44*
Rice, Grantland, 17
Rice University, 8, 41, 74, 75
Riegels, Roy, 41
Riley, Joe, 72
Rockne, Knute, 25, 26, 27, 28
Ronsonet, Norbie, 44
Rose Bowl, 18, 21, 24, 25, 29, 32, 33, 35, 41, 53, 70, 71, 72
Ross, J. P., 12
Rutledge, Gary, 53
Rutledge, Jeff, 53, *54*, 64, 68, 73
Ryba, Jim, 32

Sabo, Al, 34
Salem, Ed, *65*, 66, 67
Salls, Don, 34
Sanders, Terry, 55
Savage, Frank M. "Pops", 12, 66
Scales, Louis, 34
Scarbath, Jack, 40
Schamun, Russ, 74
Scott, Xen, 6, 15, *16*, 16, 17, 19
Sewanee, 13, 15, 24
Sewell, Joe, *15*, 15
Sewell, Luke, 15, 16, 17
Shaw, Cliff, 75
Shealy, Steadman, 53, *54*, 68
Shelly, J. E., 66
Shelton, Bobby, 67
Sherrill, Jackie, 48
Shula, David, *59*, 59, 60
Sington, Fred, 24, *25*, 25, 44
Sinkwich, Frank, 34
Skelton, Bobby, *44*, 44, 45
Sloan, Steve, 7, 43, *48*, 48, 49, 74
Smith, Dan, 12
Smith, David, 61, 62, 66
Smith, Riley, *31*, 31, *32*, 32, 71, 72
Southeastern Conference (SEC) 13, 35, 43, 53, 58, 62, 64, 69, 72

Southern Methodist University, 57
Spencer, Paul, 34
Split-T offense, 43
Stabler, Ken, 7, 43, *49*, 52, 64, 68
Stagg, Amos Alonzo, *27*, 55, 67
Stallings, Gene, 7, 62, *63*, *76*
Stanford University, 24, 29, 32, 71, 72
Starr, Bart, 39, 41
Stephenson, Riggs, 15, 16
Stock, Mike, 74
Sugar Bowl, 36, 43, 45, 46, 49, 53, 55, 71, 72, 73, 74, 75, 76, 77
Sullivan, George, 17
Sullivan, Pat, 64
Sun Bowl, 57, 59, 60, 61
Suther, John, 71
Sutton, Vince, 61
Syracuse University, 19, 39, 40, 41, 73

Tennessee, University of, 14, 15, 29, 31, 32, 34, 41, 52, 53, 58, 60, 61, 62
Tew, Lowell, 35
Texas, University of, 36, 37, 43, 48, 75, 76
Texas A&M, 34, 43, 61, 63, 75
Tharp, Corky, 39, 41
Thomas, Derrick, 8, 61, 62
Thomas, Frank, 6, 8, 26-35, *27*, *29*, 36, 37, 41, 42, 43, 45, 57, 64, 71, 72, 73, 75
Tiffin, Van, 59, *60*, 60, 68
Tillman, Lawyer, 53, 74
Todd, Richard, 53, 74
Tollett, Vaughn, 34
Trammell, Joe, 64
Trammell, Pat, 7, 43, 44, 45, 53, 67, 68, 73
Trimble, Wayne, 76
Trippi, Charlie, 35
Tulane University, 12, 21, 28, 34, 37, 44
Turner, Rory, 68

Vandegraaff, W. T. "Bully", *14*, 15
Vanderbilt University, 16, 19, 24, 32, 33, 37, 53
Vines, Melvin "Snake", 24
Virginia Tech, 39, 41, 53

Wade, John, 73
Wade, Wallace, 6, 8, 15, 17, *18*, 18-23, 26, 28, 29, 36, 42, 57, 70, 71
Wagonhurst, Otto, 13
Wahtley, Jim, *31*
Walker, Erskine, 31
Walker, M. P., 12
Warner, Glenn "Pop", 24, 27, 55
Washington, University of, 21, 53, 60, 70
Washington State University, 25, 71
Webb, Steve, *62*
Weber, Robin, 74
Welch, Clem, *65*
Wesley, Bull, 17
White, Arthur "Tarzan", 32
Whitmire, Don, 34, 75
Whitworth, J. B., 28, 36, 41
Wilkinson, Bud, 43
Williamson, Dick, 48, 75, 76
Wilson, Butch, 45
Wilson, Delma, 66
Wilson, George, 70
Winslett, Hoyt "Wu", 18, *20*, 21, 24
Wishbone offense, 43, 52, 53

Yale University, 10, 11